korean
INSTANT POT
COOKBOOK

korean
INSTANT POT
COOKBOOK

Classic and Modern Korean Recipes
for Everyday Home Cooking

NANCY CHO & SELINA LEE

Photographs by Nancy Cho

To
Raymond,
Nathan, and Tyty

&

Brad, Ben, Denise,
엄마 and 아빠

Printed in the United States of America
First Printing, 2021
ISBN Print: 978-1-7341241-2-5
ISBN Ebook: 978-1-7341241-3-2

Rocketships & Wonderment
www.rocketshipsandwonderment.com

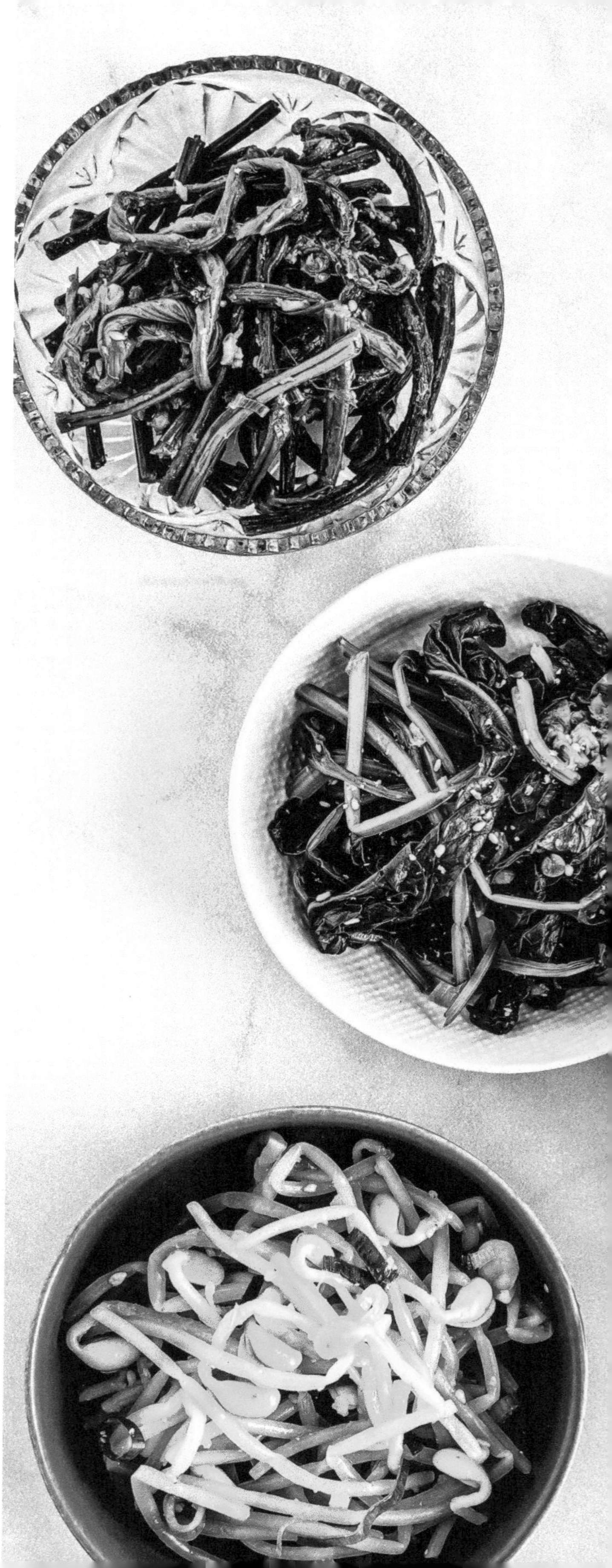

contents

introduction
밥 먹었어요?

When Nancy's book *The Easy Asian Cookbook for Slow Cookers* came out a few years ago, one question she was often asked was "When are you coming out with an Instant Pot cookbook?" She'd heard so much about this popular cooking appliance, particularly from her sister and family members, who had purchased Instant Pots for their kitchens. She wondered how this appliance could be useful for Korean recipes, especially ones known for hours-long cooking, like galbijjim and sagol gomtang. So writing a Korean cookbook one day wasn't far from her mind. As one of the first in her family to be born in the U.S., Nancy's love for cooking Korean food grew after moving out of her childhood home when she couldn't rely on her grandmother or mother to cook for her.

Selina spent her childhood in Seoul, Korea and immigrated to the U.S. when she was 12 years old. One of the ways she maintained a strong connection to her cultural roots was through Korean food, which she learned to make by helping her mother and grandmother in the kitchen. In 2014, she started offering Korean cooking classes in San Francisco called Banchan Workshop featuring classic and modern recipes. The series of classes became popular among second generation children of Korean immigrants and Korean-food lovers alike. It eventually led to her becoming a consultant for restaurants, developing recipes and menus.

It was at one of her Banchan Workshop cooking classes where Nancy and Selina met. Nancy was taking the class to expand her knowledge of Korean cooking. They bonded over their mutual appreciation for traditional techniques and their favorite dish, naengmyeon. They both lamented over their inability to find a great naengmyeon place where they lived, and gabbed for hours, dreaming about opening up a little lunch place and making their version of the dish.

At the time, Selina was dedicated to learning traditional Korean cooking methods—often lengthy processes—so initially she wasn't as interested in using the Instant Pot. But she did recall that as a young child, her mother made rice, braised meats, and fish in their old pressure cooker, and fondly remembered the train noise that the cooker would make.

• • •

During the Covid-19 pandemic, we found ourselves cooking a lot more at home, like many folks. We realized that using the Instant Pot was very helpful in getting food on the table fast and easy. Complicated dishes that required a lot of work and time were simpler to make, diversified our weekly dinner menus, and satisfied our cravings. Once the food was cooking inside the pot, there was no having to stir, monitor, or adjust cooking temperatures. And since our children were always at home, it became a great opportunity to teach our kids how to cook Korean food with the Instant Pot (especially with Selina's child getting ready to go off to college in a couple years). Together, we started sharing and geeking out over our recipe successes, which ultimately led to the cookbook you now have in your hands!

about the book

This book features many of our favorite and classic recipes. Pressure cooking lends itself well to making so many staples in Korean cuisine like soups, stews, braised meats, rice and jook. With the Instant Pot, you can do more than just pressure cooking, so you will find that some recipes will be using a variety of functions like sauté, steam, and even sous vide with some models. For easy reference, each recipe includes:

- Serving Size
- Estimated Prep Time
- Pressure Cook Time
- Release Method

Almost all the recipes serve 4 to 6 people, and every single one was tried and tested by us on the Instant Pot Duo Evo Plus 6-Quart Pressure Cooker. You will find that most of the recipes in the Banchan and the Sauces chapters do not use the Instant Pot, but are simple enough to make while a main dish is cooking in your Instant Pot. There are also tips and suggestions in the recipes, and a Glossary (page 162) to learn more about ingredients and any substitutions.

korean table
밥상

In Korean culture, the table where you eat your meals is called bapsang. The Korean diet primarily consists of legumes, fish, meat, and fresh, fermented, or cooked vegetables. Traditionally, red meat was not a highly-consumed food because of limited livestock farming and subsequent high cost. Although the table can vary according to the occasion, the common person's day-to-day bapsang usually contains rice, soup or stew, kimchi, and banchan. Rice is a staple and the main dietary energy source. A soup or stew accompanies a meal to help in digestion. Banchan, the small side dishes, are meant to be shared. You can have very little or numerous amounts of banchan at the table.

One of the ways to avoid food spoiling during hot summers or long and brutal winters, was using the fermentation process to preserve food. Koreans made various jang (sauce made from fermented soy blocks) in order to flavor their food. There are many different kinds of jang, but the most common ones for seasoning are ganjang (soy sauce), doenjang (soybean paste), and gochujang (red pepper paste). Sometimes, you will find jang on the table to flavor food and it is meant to help boost one's appetite.

Here's what can be found in an everyday bapsang:

- *Grain*: Usually rice or barley
- *Guk or Jjigae*: Soup or stew
- *Kimchi*: Fermented cabbage served at every meal
- *Banchan 1*: Protein dish that could be fish or meat
- *Banchan 2*: Namul, a seasoned side dish typically made from vegetables, greens, roots, herbs, and stems
- *Banchan 3*: Small side dish or namul

korean kitchen

As Korean food increases in popularity, more and more grocery stores are stocking ingredients used in Korean cooking. Combined with online sources like H Mart (hmart.com) and Seoul Mills (seoulmills.com), you can find most ingredients needed for a nicely-stocked Korean pantry. Although there are many other ingredients used in Korean cooking, the following are commonly-used ingredients we use and keep in our pantries.

If you are unfamiliar with any of the ingredients in the recipes, you can find more info listed in the Glossary (page 162).

sauces and oils

Cheongju 청주 (rice wine). A Korean clear liquor beverage made from rice, it is often used for marinades, sauces, and seasoning. It also helps to reduce gaminess in meat and fish. If you can't find cheongju, you can substitute with soju or cooking sake, a Japanese rice wine that is found in most major super markets.

Doenjang 된장 (fermented soybean paste). One of the three major jangs (sauces) used in Korean cooking, doenjang is a fermented soybean paste made from soybeans and salt, and fermented for months. Doenjang is thick, salty, nutty, sharp, and a bit funky. This one sauce packs a punch with complex and incredible deep flavors.

Ganjang 간장 (soy sauce). Ganjang is made from fermented soybeans, a roasted grain, and salt. Traditionally, ganjang used to be made only from soybeans, water, and salt, but now most use some sort of grain like wheat. Ganjang used in Korean cooking comes in various types. The ones we use most in this book are ganjang (standard soy sauce) and guk ganjang (soup soy sauce).

Gochujang 고추장 (red chili pepper paste). Gochujang is a red chili paste made of Korean chili powder, fermented soybean powder, glutinous sweet rice powder, and salt. Gochujang is spicy, slightly pungent, sweet, and very bold. You can purchase it in different levels of spice ranging from mild to super hot.

Guk ganjang 국간장 (soup soy sauce). Yes, there's another type of soy sauce that is essential to a Korean kitchen. Guk ganjang (soup soy sauce), a byproduct of doenjang, is lighter in color and saltier than regular soy sauce. It is very strong and bold in flavor, so it is good to use in seasoning soups and stews.

Mirin 미림 (cooking wine). A cooking wine similar to cheongju and sake, it has a lower alcohol content and contains more sugar. It is often used in marinades to help tenderize meat and adds a hint of tang and sweetness to dishes. For a substitution, mix a 3:1 ratio of sake and sugar together.

Sesame oil 참기름. Made from sesame seeds, sesame oil has a fragrant and distinct flavor, so it can go a long way. Although it is used for cooking food, it is also often used at the end of cooking to enhance flavor in a dish.

dried staples

Anchovies/Kelp dry stock bags or dashi pack 멸치다시팩.
A stock bag filled with precut myeolchi (dried anchovies) and
dashima (dried kelp), sometimes containing small dried shrimp.
This can be a luxury purchase, but it's convenient and a big time
saver! Removing one bag from a stock pot is much easier than
fishing out loose myeolchi bits! (You can make your own stock
bags with myeolchi and dashima in a large strainer bag or tied up
in cheesecloth.)

Dashima 다시마 **(dried kelp).** Sheets of dried kelp that usually
come in large sheets that you have to cut, or precut swatches
are also available. Dashima adds a rich and salty depth of
flavor to broths. It is often labeled at Asian markets as kombu
(in Japanese). Dashima and myeolchi are important ingredients
for Korean stocks. Make a vegetarian version using dashima and
dried shiitake mushrooms.

Dried shiitake mushrooms 표고버섯. Dried shiitake mushrooms
add a more complex, earthy, and rich flavor to dishes and stocks.
You can't substitute them with the fresh ones because the flavor
becomes more intense when dried.

Gochugaru 고춧가루 **(red chili pepper flakes).** Fine or
coarsely ground, deseeded sun-dried Korean red chili
peppers. We prefer gochugaru made in Korea because the
flavor is so distinct, less bitter, a little sweeter, and the color
is bright red. There's no real substitute for gochugaru. When
we list gochugaru in the ingredients, we are referring to
coarse gochugaru. Gochugaru powder (finely ground
gochugaru) is specified in the ingredients list.

Myeolchi 멸치 **(dried anchovies).** Dried anchovies that come in different sizes. Large myeolchi
are used for making broths (see Man Neung
Myeolchi Yooksu, page 139) and the smaller ones
are typically used to make banchan. Discard the
heads and black innards from large myeolchi before using them or they will leave a
bitter taste. You don't need to do this
to small myeolchi; their size will not
affect flavor.

produce

Dae pa 대파 (bunching onion). Dae pa looks like a very large scallion, but it is sweeter and more fragrant in taste. It is used to flavor soups and stews and very different from leeks, so do not use it as a substitute. If you cannot find dae pa, use regular scallions.

Garlic 마늘. Okay, we know you are familiar with garlic, but we have to mention it because it's in nearly everything. We even eat it sliced raw, for crying out loud. We use so much that we mince, grind, or pound it in large batches to freeze. (Spread prepped raw garlic into a thin layer in a freezer bag and freeze. It makes it fast and easy to break off when cooking.)

Gochu 고추 (Korean green & red chili peppers). Korean chili peppers that are green or red and vary in heat level, so taste and test the heat

before cooking with them. They are usually about 3 to 4 inches long with pointy ends. When the green ones ripen, they turn red on the vine.

Mu 무 (Korean radish). Korean radishes are large and firm. They are pale green at the top and fade to a white color. If you cannot find mu, substitute with daikon. Mu is heavier, spicier, and has more water content than daikon. Mu is available all year round in Korean markets, but most flavorful when mu is in season during the fall.

Napa cabbage 배추. An oblong-shaped cabbage used in kimchi, soups, dumplings, and wraps. You'll want to pick out a leafy cabbage head that is green and heavy, with thin leaves. It is also known as Chinese cabbage or celery cabbage, and widely used in East Asian cuisine.

south korea regional dishes

During most of the Joseon Dynasty, Korea was divided into eight provinces, determined by mountains and rivers, and regional distinctions, like dialects. These eight major provinces, Pal-do, refer to Korea as a whole. The Korean War divided the country and formed more provinces, though the original eight provinces in South Korea are still preserved to some degree today. South Korea has nine provinces with distinct cuisine styles. The following list describes some dishes and characteristics unique to each region in South Korea:

GYEONGGI-DO/SEOUL (경기도/서울). *Galbitang, janchi guksu, seolleongtang, tteokguk, yukgaejang.* Dishes are not overly seasoned and portion sizes are smaller, with more variety at the table. There is an emphasis on visual presentation. The sea is on the west and mountains on the east, providing a perfect climate for a bounty of ingredients. Most dishes were popularized by the royal courts.

CHOONGCHEUNG-DO (충청도) NORTH/SOUTH. *Barley rice, hobac jook, kalguksu, rice cake varieties.* There are plenty of grains due to the rich agriculture, resulting in a variety of rice cakes. The regional seafood comes from the west sea. Dishes don't include a lot of seasoning and many feature ginseng. The food is very modest and natural.

GANGWON-DO (강원도). *Dakgalbi, dotori mook, gamjabap, maemil guksu, ojinguh soondae.* Surrounded by mountain terrain, this region cultivates namul (plants) like potatoes, corn, acorn, and buckwheat. The sea is on the east side, providing plenty of seafood. The dishes are simple and modest, clean and light.

GYEONGSANG-DO (경상도) NORTH/SOUTH. *Ahgujjim, andong jjimdak, chuhtang, pa kimchi.* The hot and humid climate of this region produces bountiful crops and seafood. Many dishes use a lot of gochugaru and salt for seasoning.

JEOLLA-DO (전라도) NORTH/SOUTH. *Bibimbap, kongnamul gukbap, soonchang gochujang.* This region is famous for originating bibimbap and known for massive table settings filled with numerous banchan. Gochugaru and jeotgal (salted seafood) are used to season many dishes. The food is salty, spicy, and packed with gamchilmat (umami).

JEJU-DO (제주도). *Black pork, galchi, gamgyul, jun bok jook.* This island produces beans and barley. It boasts seafood and sea plants, and surprisingly, meat as well (beef, pork, and chicken). The cuisine is known for using doenjang as a seasoning agent, and preserving natural flavors.

instant pot basics

pressure cooking

Pressure cooking is the process of cooking food in an airtight vessel. When the chamber is sealed and heating the trapped air inside, it creates steam and builds pressure. As the pressure grows, the boiling point of the water also increases so the liquid inside can reach a temperature higher than 212°F. What does this all mean? The boiling point at sea level is 212°F and the pressure cooker goes beyond that temperature. which means that you can use a pressure cooker to braise or simmer food in a much shorter amount of time.

High Pressure Mode. The High Pressure mode typically sets your Instant Pot to reach a pressure range between 10 to 12 psi (pounds per square inch). This brings your cooking temperature to a range between 239°F to 245°F. Depending on your model, your Instant Pot can go as high as 15 psi.

Low Pressure Mode. The Low Pressure mode sets your Instant Pot to reach a pressure range between 5.5 to 7.2 psi. This brings your cooking temperature to a range between 229°F to 233°F.

Float Valve. The float valve is a silver or red metal pin next to the steam valve. When your cooker is fully pressurized, the valve will float up. When the cooker is no longer pressurized, the valve drops and you can safely open the cooker.

Natural Release. When cooking is complete, the Instant Pot will release air and cool down naturally until the float valve drops. Depending on how much food is inside the pot, this can take an average of 10 to 40 minutes. Since the pressure is gradually released, there will be less movement inside the pot.

Quick Release. When cooking is complete, you can manually release the pressure all at once by switching the quick-release valve to venting. When all the steam has released, the float valve will drop down. We use quick release to avoid overcooking delicate foods like vegetables and seafood. Quick release is not usually recommended for cooking in large volume or for high starch contents like rice and beans.

tools & equipment

Trivet. Most Instant Pots come with a trivet, a raised platform so that your food or cookware, like a small pot or baking pan, doesn't rest directly on the bottom of the inner pot. This comes in handy for steaming foods like large vegetables or for recipes that call for food to be cooked in a bowl or pan. There are a variety of steam racks available for purchase, including some made of silicone and others lined handles. Stackable and tall trivets are also available for purchase.

Tempered Glass Lid. Tempered glass lids can be used when slow cooking, sautéing, or keeping food warm in the Instant Pot. It's handy to see your food and to avoid anything from splattering. It is also nice to use the lid when storing food in the refrigerator.

Extra Silicone Sealing Rings. You may notice that your silicone sealing ring will absorb the smells from foods cooked. Even though they can develop odors, it should not transfer to the dishes you cook. But, just in case, we like to keep one sealing ring for savory foods and one for sweets. In addition, the sealing rings don't last forever, so you might as well have extras on hand.

Steaming Basket. A steaming basket is handy for holding vegetables, eggs, or any foods that need steaming. We don't use the basket a lot in this book, but it is nice to have if you need to separate and contain foods from being cooked in liquid.

Silicone Lid. Okay, so you have the tempered glass lid...do you really need a silicone lid? We admit, this one is kind of a luxury item, but we love it. This lid creates an airtight and watertight seal on the inner pot, which is great for storing and transporting food.

Extra Inner Pot. Having an extra inner pot is helpful when you want to cook multiple dishes (like rice plus a main dish), or when one pot is occupied and storing food.

Ttukbaegi (Korean Earthenware Pot). A clay-based cooking vessel that retains heat and does not cool quickly. Frequently used for many Korean dishes, ttukbaegi are great for keeping soups and stews warm at the table. Ttukbaegi are Instant Pot-safe, but make sure to place a trivet underneath and add at least 1 cup of water to the inner pot before cooking.

Immersion Blender. A handheld kitchen tool used to blend soups, sauces, and other liquids. Instead of having to transfer liquids to a regular blender, you can use an immersion blender to blend foods inside the cooking pot.

Blender. You will need to use a traditional blender to purée some foods in this book. If you do not own an immersion blender, you can use a blender.

Fine Mesh Skimmer. A super-fine mesh skimmer helps remove foamy scum and impurities on the surface of soups and broths. An online search for "Hot Pot Fat Skimmer Spoon" can help you find a super fine mesh skimmer.

frequently asked questions

Which Instant Pot model should I get?

Currently, six Instant Pot models are available. Most of the recipes in this book use the basic functions, so you should be covered with whatever model you have or choose to get. The fancier you go up in the Instant Pot food chain, the more features you'll get. We used the Duo Evo Plus, which seemed like the middle ground between all the models while still having many options and presets.

- *Lux Series.* This is the baseline model and a starter pressure cooker. It has six program modes and the only model without a low-pressure option. For recipes that call for low pressure, manually lower and adjust your cooking time.
- *Duo Plus Series.* Great for beginners and includes most functions you need, such as low and high pressure cooking and sauté functions.
- *Ultra Series.* Upgraded and includes special features from Duo Plus Series, including more control over temperature settings. The temperature can be specified to the degree ranging from 104°F to 208°F.

How much liquid do I need?

Well, the rule of thumb for new users is to start with at least 1 cup of liquid. But, if you find a recipe that says otherwise, then follow the recipe instructions. Some recipes will call for very little liquid because it accounts for the released liquid during cooking. But when in doubt, use at least 1 cup.

How full can I fill the pot?

For most dishes, do not go past the PC Max line. However, when cooking foods that expand, like rice and beans, don't fill the pot past the ½ line or else you'll risk the unit from turning off or boiling over. That said, if you are cooking something in a bowl with a trivet inside the inner pot (the pot-in-pot cooking method), like Gyeran Jjim (page 33), then it is okay to go over the PC Max line.

How long does it take to cook?

The pressure-cooking times listed in this book exclude pressurizing and pressure release times. In general, account 5 to 30 minutes for pressurizing time, and about 5 to 30 minutes for pressure to release after cooking. In this book, recipes take an average of 5 to 15 minutes to pressurize and 5 to 15 minutes to depressurize. Keep in mind that timing depends on the amount of food, liquid in the pot, and ingredient temperatures. For instance, if you put frozen ingredients in the pot, it will take longer to cook.

Ugh, my sealing ring stinks! How can I get rid of the odor?

It's nice to have a ring for savory dishes and a separate one for sweets. If you only have one, try some of these tips:

- Run it in the dishwasher. The rings are dishwasher safe, so put it on your top rack and wash.

- Make solution of equal parts vinegar and water and soak your silicone ring overnight.
- Add two cups of white vinegar to your Instant Pot and run it on the Steam setting for 2 minutes. When complete, remove the ring and let it dry completely.

Does the cooking time change if I double the recipe?

The cooking time remains the same, but your pressurizing and depressurizing time will increase as the food portions increase. As long as the pot does not overflow, you can double the recipe.

My Instant Pot doesn't have a Manual button. What should I do?

Some Instant Pots have a Manual button, but not all. Don't worry, set to Pressure Cook and select High or Low; it's the same function.

What about high altitude cooking?

Pressure cooking at altitudes below 2000 feet do not need to be adjusted. Remember: the higher the altitude, the longer the cooking. Liquid's boiling point is lower at higher altitudes, so if you are at altitudes higher than 2000 feet, adjust your cooking time by using the chart in the Cooking Tables (page 166).

1
banchan

Geotjeori, page 20

geotjeori
겉절이김치
fresh napa cabbage kimchi
20

kkaennip jjim
깻잎찜
seasoned perilla leaves
21

samsaek namul
삼색나물
seasoned spinach, soybean sprouts, & fernbrake
23

jangjorim
장조림
soy-braised beef
25

myeolchi bokkeum
멸치볶음
stir-fried dried anchovies
27

oi mak kimchi
오이막김치
quick cucumber kimchi
28

chwinamul
취나물
stir-fried aster scaber
30

mayak gyeran
마약계란
marinated eggs
31

gyeran jjim
계란찜
steamed eggs
33

gaji namul
가지나물
seasoned eggplant
34

gamja salad
감자 샐러드
korean-style potato salad
35

kong ja ban
콩자반
soy-braised black beans
36

dubu jorim
두부조림
spicy seasoned tofu
38

maneul jjong
마늘쫑
stir-fried garlic stems
39

geotjeori 겉절이김치

fresh napa cabbage kimchi

Makes 6 cups

The idea of making homemade kimchi may seem daunting. It is an ordeal that requires planning and prepping which is why I usually resort to store-bought kimchi. But lately, I've gotten into the rhythm of making small batches of kimchi at home. I make sure to have all the staple pantry ingredients so I can make it whenever fresh ingredients are available. This fresh napa cabbage kimchi does not require any fermentation and can be eaten on the same day. - *Selina*

Prep Time / 12 min, plus 2 to 4 hrs to brine

Cook Time / 0 min

1 (2 lb) small napa cabbage head

3 (1 lb) large choy sum

½ cup plus 2 tbsp fine sea salt

2 tbsp gochugaru

2 tbsp gochugaru powder

1 tbsp minced garlic

1 tsp ginger juice

1 tbsp white granulated sugar

1 tbsp fish sauce

1 tbsp brown rice vinegar

¼ cup grated apple

1 Cut the cabbage in half. Core and remove the stem from the base of each cabbage half. Pull apart and separate the cabbage leaves. Cut the leaves lengthwise so they are roughly ½-inch wide. Cut into 3- to 4-inch long pieces. Remove choy sum stems and separate each leaf. Cut into ½-inch wide pieces.

2 In a large bowl, mix 1 cup water and 2 tablespoons sea salt, and add the cabbage and choy sum. In a small bowl, add ½ cup of sea salt. By the pinchful, sprinkle salt evenly over the top layer of cabbage and choy sum. Cover the bowl with a tea towel. Let it sit for 2 to 4 hours to brine the cabbage. Turn over the cabbage and choy sum every hour until soft.

3 In a small bowl, add the gochugaru, gochugaru powder, garlic, ginger juice, sugar, fish sauce, vinegar, and grated apple. Mix until well-combined.

4 Quickly rinse the brine from the cabbage and choy sum in running water and squeeze out some of the excess liquid by hand, then place in a large mixing bowl..

5 Thoroughly massage the seasoning into the cabbage and choy sum.

6 Can be served on the same day, or for more mature flavors, store in fridge for 2 to 3 days before eating.

kkaennip jjim 깻잎찜

seasoned perilla leaves

Serves 4

Kkaennip leaves are my favorite Korean herb. It's often spotted on the Korean bapsang as a pickled banchan or fresh, alongside lettuce wraps at Korean BBQ. It is wonderfully fragrant and adds a hint of freshness. It falls under a mint family and is similar to shiso leaves, but a little tougher in texture. When my children were young, a Korean caregiver would come to our home to help care for them. She would sometimes bring kkaennip jjim for my husband and me to eat with our meals. Her seasoned kkaennip were steamed, making them much more tender than the ones typically bought at the market. You take a leaf and wrap it around a scoop of fresh, steaming rice. It's a tasty mouthful. - *Selina*

Prep Time / 10 min
Cook Time / 10 min

½ cup soy sauce

2 garlic cloves, minced

2 scallions, thinly sliced

1 tsp gochugaru

1 tbsp perilla oil

1 Korean green chili pepper, minced

1 Korean red chili pepper, minced

1 tbsp roasted sesame seeds

2 bundles kkaennip (perilla) leaves

1 In a small bowl, combine 4 tablespoons water, soy sauce, garlic, scallions, gochugaru, perilla oil, green and red chili peppers, and sesame seeds.

2 Stack the kkaennip leaves in one direction, holding the stack by the stems with one hand over a bowl, and apply seasoning with a spoon on each layer of leaves. Place kkaennip in an Instant Pot safe bowl, pour any remaining seasoning over them.

3 Add 2 cups of water into the inner pot then place the steamer rack. Place the bowl with kkaennip inside.

4 Turn and lock the lid in place with the steam release valve into a sealed position. Select Steam function, then program for 10 minutes. Unlock and carefully remove the lid then remove the bowl.

5 Allow to cool, then serve. Store in the refrigerator for up to 5 to 7 days.

samsaek namul 삼색나물

seasoned spinach, soybean sprouts, & fernbrake

Makes about 2 cups per banchan

Samsaek translates to "tricolor," and these banchan, sigeumchi namul (seasoned spinach), kongnamul muchim (seasoned soybean sprouts), and gosari namul (seasoned fernbrake), are often the most common ones on a Korean dining table. They are great as stand-alone side dishes. Use these three classic banchan to make bibimbap (see "Making Bibimbap," page 24). - *Nancy*

Prep Time / 38 min
Pressure Cook Time / 5 min
Cook Time / 10 min
Release / Quick

SIGEUMCHI NAMUL 시금치나물

¾ **lb spinach, stems trimmed**

1 **scallion, thinly sliced**

1 **tsp minced garlic**

1 ½ **tsp soy sauce**

1 **tsp sesame oil**

1 **tsp roasted sesame seeds**

KONGNAMUL MUCHIM 콩나물 무침

1 **lb soybean sprouts**

1 **tsp kosher salt**

1 **scallion, thinly sliced**

1 **tsp minced garlic**

1 **tsp roasted sesame seeds**

1½ **tsp sesame oil**

GOSARI NAMUL 고사리 나물

1 **oz dried gosari (fernbrake), rinsed and drained**

2 **tsp guk ganjang (soup soy sauce)**

1 **tsp minced garlic**

1 **scallion, thinly sliced**

1 **tbsp vegetable oil**

¼ **cup rice water (see Glossary, page 165), or plain water**

½ **tsp sesame oil**

1 **tsp roasted sesame seeds, roughly ground**

To make Sigeumchi Namul

1 Bring a large pot of water to boil and blanch the spinach for about 20 seconds.

2 Quickly drain the spinach and rinse thoroughly in very cold water and drain well. Gently squeeze out excess water by hand and transfer to a large bowl.

3 Add scallion, garlic, soy sauce, sesame oil, and sesame seeds to the spinach. Mix well together while gently loosening any clumps of spinach by hand.

4 Add salt to taste and serve.

Tip Use baby spinach to save time. Blanch baby spinach for about 10 seconds.

To make Kongnamul Muchim

1 Fill a large bowl with cold water and add soybean sprouts. Discard floating soybean skins and kernel shells, and remove rotten or browned soybean sprouts. Drain water, rinse, and drain well.

2 In a large pot, add 1½ cups of water, kosher salt, and soybean sprouts. Cover the pot and boil over medium heat for about 7 minutes. Do not open the lid.

3 Drain the sprouts into a large colander and rinse thoroughly with cold water. Remove any excess water.

(recipe continues)

samsaek namul

삼색나물

seasoned spinach, soybean sprouts, & fernbrake (continued)

4 Transfer soybean sprouts to a bowl. Add scallions, garlic, sesame seeds, and sesame oil. Mix together by hand to evenly coat the sprouts.

5 Add salt to taste and serve.

To make Gosari Namul

1 Place gosari in the inner pot and pour enough hot water in the pot to cover the gosari.

2 Turn and lock the lid and move the steam release valve to the sealed position. Select Pressure Cook on High and program for 5 minutes. When the cooking is complete, quick-release pressure manually and press Cancel.

3 Place gosari in a colander, rinse in cold water and drain. Sort through gosari and remove any tough stems. Roughly cut gosari into 3- to 4-inch lengths and transfer to a bowl.

4 Add guk ganjang, garlic, and scallion to gosari and mix well.

5 Heat a frying pan over medium-high heat and add vegetable oil. When the oil is shimmering, add gosari and stir-fry for about 2 minutes.

6 Add rice water to the pan. Lower the heat to medium and cook until the liquid has almost evaporated, about 3 to 4 minutes.

7 Turn the heat off. Stir in sesame oil and sesame seeds and serve.

making bibimbap

Bibimbap means "mixed rice" and can be made with a variety of ingredients. Assemble bibimbap using these three classic banchan. Start by adding a serving of rice in a large serving bowl. Place preferred amount of sigeumchi, kongnamul, and gosari namul on top of rice. Add a fried egg and protein of choice like fried tofu, grilled chicken, or Maple Syrup Bulgogi (page 98). Serve with Bibimjang (page 154) at the table. Drizzle bibimjang over rice bowl, mix together, and enjoy!

jangjorim 장조림

soy-braised beef

Serves 4 to 6

Jangjorim is one of my favorite banchan. As a kid, if I was hungry after school, I would grab some kimchi and jangjorim out of the fridge and eat it with a bowl of rice. Thirty plus years later, I still do this. I like to wrap bite-sized jangjorim pieces with individual gim (roasted seaweed) sheets and rice, and also enjoy eating it with jook, adding small spoonfuls of the sauce. Even though it's a side dish, adding hard-boiled eggs can make it a pretty nice meal. - *Nancy*

Prep Time / 15 min, plus 30 min to soak
Pressure Cook Time / 40 min
Release / Quick

1 to 1½ lbs beef brisket, cut into 2-inch wide pieces

¾ cup soy sauce

¼ cup white granulated sugar

1 (3-inch long) dashima (dried kelp)

½ small mu (Korean radish), peeled and cut in half

1 small onion, cut in half

2 scallion stems (white part only)

½ cup garlic cloves, divided

1 tsp black peppercorns (optional)

10 small shishito peppers

4 hard-boiled eggs, peeled (optional, see page 31)

1 Soak beef in cold water for 30 minutes to help drain the blood.

2 Drain beef and transfer to the inner cooking pot. Add 2 cups water, soy sauce, sugar, dashima, mu, onion, scallion stems, 3 garlic cloves, and a strainer bag with black peppercorns (see Tip).

3 Turn and lock the lid and move the steam release valve to the sealed position. Select the Meat setting on High and program for 40 minutes. When the cooking is complete, quick-release manually. Unlock and carefully remove the lid.

4 Using a skimmer, discard the strainer bag, dashima, mu, onion, and scallion stems. Press Sauté on High for 10 minutes.

5 Add the remaining garlic cloves, shishito peppers, and hard-boiled eggs (if using), stirring periodically.

6 After 8 to 10 minutes, when the peppers have turned to a darker green and the garlic is tender, press Cancel and transfer the meat to a cutting board. Once the beef is cool enough to touch, shred the beef by hand or with a fork.

(recipe continues).

jangjorim
장조림
soy-braised beef
(continued)

7 Serve beef on a dish with peppers, eggs, garlic, and ladle sauce over, or transfer into an airtight container submerging the beef and eggs in the sauce and refrigerate to serve cold later.

Tip Use strainer bags for small ingredients like garlic and peppercorns so that they will be easier to take out.

myeolchi bokkeum 멸치볶음

stir-fried dried anchovies

Serves 4 (banchan servings)

Myeolchi bokkeum is my son's favorite banchan. He loves the salty, sweet toasty tiny fishes. I used to pack these tiny fishes in his lunch box with some rice and toasted seaweed. He once told me that his friends at school stared intently at his food and some remarked, "Eww, that's gross." I asked him if he felt embarrassed. He proudly told me, "No." He didn't feel embarrassed at all and said his friends simply were missing out on delicious food. Let's just say this was my proudest moment as a Korean-American mom. - *Selina*

Prep Time / 0 min
Cook Time / 7 min

- 1 tbsp cooking oil
- ½ cup jan myeolchi (tiny dried anchovies)
- 2 tbsp sliced almonds
- 1 tbsp low sodium soy sauce
- 1 tbsp white granulated sugar
- 1 tsp honey
- 1 tsp sesame oil
- ½ tsp roasted sesame seeds

1 In a medium sauté pan, add cooking oil over medium-low heat. Once the pan is warm, sauté myeolchi and sliced almonds for about 5 minutes until toasty brown.

2 Add soy sauce around the edge of the pan then lower the heat.

3 Add sugar and honey. Toss using two spatulas or wooden spoons in each hand. Turn the heat off and add sesame oil and roasted sesame seeds. Stir until well-combined.

4 Allow to cool, then serve.

Tip Using more honey than sugar will harden the glaze. Use more sugar to preserve toastiness and shelf life in the refrigerator.

oi mak kimchi 오이막김치

quick cucumber kimchi

Serves 8

Oi mak kimchi is a type of kimchi that goes well with pretty much any Korean dish. Mak means rustic or rough. In this instance, it can be interpreted as quick or easy. Living in California, I feel lucky to have access to a wide variety of fresh cucumbers all year round. I prefer Persian cucumbers for this kimchi. - *Selina*

Prep Time / 30 min
Cook Time / 0 min

7 to 8 Persian cucumbers, quartered and cut into 2-inch pieces

1 tbsp fine sea salt

½ small mu (Korean radish), peeled and cut into 2-inch matchsticks

¼ lb garlic chives

1 large carrot, cut into 2-inch matchsticks (optional)

1 scallion, cut into 2-inch pieces (optional)

KIMCHI SEASONING

4 tbsp gochugaru

2 tbsp gochugaru powder

1 tbsp minced garlic

1 tsp grated ginger or ginger juice

1 tbsp white granulated sugar

1 tbsp fish sauce

1 tbsp plum extract syrup

Special equipment: fermentation weight or small heavyweight item

1 With a metal spoon, roughly remove cucumber seeds. Sprinkle sea salt evenly and let it brine in a large bowl for 15 to 30 minutes.

2 Remove all the liquid from the cucumbers and add mu, chives, carrots (if using) and scallion (if using). Set aside.

3 In a mixing bowl, whisk all seasoning ingredients with ¼ cup water until well-combined and paste-like.

4 Add the kimchi seasoning paste to the bowl with cucumbers and mu. Combine well.

5 Oi mak kimchi must be tightly sealed at this stage for proper fermentation. To prevent air from entering or escaping, place kimchi in an airtight container. The kimchi should sit neatly in and fill the storage vessel. If there is extra space in the container, use a fermentation weight or a small heavyweight item to weigh the kimchi down and limit it from being exposed to air.

6 Refrigerate for 2 to 3 days before serving.

Tip For a sugar alternative, use fruit pureé such as Asian pear or apple.

chwinamul 취나물

stir-fried aster scaber

Serves 4

I often wander through the dried ingredient aisle in the Korean market thinking excitedly, What can I make with these dried veggies? Koreans traditionally dry vegetables to last through the long winters. A simple way to bring life to these dried vegetables is to soak and expand them in water, then season with fragrant aromatics like sesame or perilla oils. I love the earthy taste of chwinamul when it's been sautéed with garlic, salt, and perilla oil. - *Selina*

Prep Time / 5 min
Pressure Cook Time / 5 min
Release / Quick

2 cups dried chwinamul (aster scaber)

5 garlic cloves, minced

1 tbsp perilla oil

1 tsp perilla seed powder

½ tsp kosher salt

1 tsp soy sauce

1 Using a colander, rinse the dried chwinamul under cool running water several times. Remove dirt and any hard or tough brown pieces.

2 Add chwinamul and 6 cups of water to the inner pot.

3 Turn and lock the lid and move the steam release valve to the sealed position. Select Pressure Cook on High and program for 5 minutes. When the cooking is complete, quick-release pressure manually. Unlock and carefully remove the lid.

4 Using a skimmer, remove the chwinamul. Place in a colander and rinse using cold water. Gently squeeze excess liquid from chwinamul by hand. Using scissors, roughly cut chwinamul into 2-inch pieces.

5 In a small bowl, add chwinamul, garlic, perilla oil, perilla seed powder, kosher salt, and soy sauce. Gently mix by hand.

6 In a medium skillet over high heat, sauté chwinamul, about 2 to 3 minutes until the garlic and perilla oil is toasted and blended well.

Tip Use sesame oil and sesame seed powder as a substitute for perilla oil and perilla seed powder.

mayak gyeran 마약계란

marinated eggs

Makes 6 eggs

Okaaaaay, so the literal translation of this side dish is "drug eggs," or what I like to call, "dope eggs." And no, there's no trace of narcotics in them, but they're addictive, hence the name. I like to slice an egg in half, put it over a warm bowl of rice and spoon a little bit of the sauce on top. This is an easy breakfast for me. And lunch. And dinner. I told you, addictive. - *Nancy*

Prep Time / 15 min, plus marinating time

Pressure Cook Time / 3 to 5 min

Release / Quick

6 large eggs

⅓ cup soy sauce

¼ cup oligodang (sweet syrup)

3 scallions, thinly sliced

1 red jalapeño pepper, minced

1 serrano pepper, minced

1 tbsp minced garlic

1 tbsp roasted sesame seeds

To make hard-boiled eggs

1 Place the trivet in the inner cooking pot and add 1 cup of water. Place the eggs on the trivet without stacking on top of each other.

2 Turn and lock the lid in place with the steam release valve into the sealed position. For a hard-boiled egg, select Pressure Cook on High and program for 5 minutes. For a jammy egg, select Pressure Cook on High and program for 3 minutes.

3 In a medium bowl, prepare an ice bath with cold water and ice.

4 When the cooking is complete, quick-release pressure manually. Unlock and carefully remove the lid. Immediately transfer the eggs to the ice bath.

To season eggs

1 In a medium bowl, mix ⅓ cup water, soy sauce, oligodang, scallions, peppers, garlic, and roasted sesame seeds together until well combined.

2 Peel the eggs and place in an airtight container. Pour the sauce over the eggs, cover, and keep in the refrigerator for at least 6 hours to overnight.

3 Serve the eggs with rice and drizzle sauce over them.

gyeran jjim 계란찜

steamed eggs

Serves 2

Steamed egg is a quick side dish addition for our family dinners. It complements most main dishes and also works as a good counter-balance for any super-spicy dishes. The Instant Pot makes this dish smooth and silky, almost like a custard. Plus: no need to babysit the stove. It comes out perfectly cooked, every time. Adding shrimp or preserved pollock roe really elevate this dish. - *Selina*

Prep Time / 10 min
Steam Cook Time / 15 min
Release / None

6 large eggs
sesame oil
½ tsp fine sea salt
⅓ cup chopped shrimp
1 scallion, thinly sliced

Special equipment: small ttukbaegi (Korean earthenware pot)

1 In a small bowl, whisk the eggs or mix with a small blender. Set aside.

2 Place the steamer rack in the inner pot and add 2 cups of water.

3 Add a few drops of sesame oil to coat the bottom of the small ttukbaegi. Add the egg mixture and 1 cup of water, then season with sea salt. Add the shrimp and scallion.

4 Gently place the ttukbaegi on the steamer rack, without the ttukbaegi lid.

5 Turn and lock the lid in place with the steam release valve to the sealed position. Select the Steam setting and program for 15 minutes. When the cooking is complete, unlock and carefully remove the lid.

6 With oven mitts, carefully remove the ttukbaegi from the Instant Pot and place on a trivet. Serve directly in the ttukbaegi for sharing.

Tips

- Using a blender to whisk the eggs will make a smoother mixture.

- For a ttukbaegi alternative, use a microwave-safe bowl that can resist high heat.

- Instead of shrimp, use ¼ cup myeongran jeot (preserved pollock roe) with the skin removed.

gaji namul 가지나물

seasoned eggplant

Serves 4 to 6

I've been reintroducing myself to vegetables I like but don't often pick up at the grocery or farmers' markets. I tend to buy the same vegetables and keep them on a standard rotation in my kitchen. In an effort to eat more seasonal vegetables, I discovered eggplant can be used in many different Korean dishes. This is a classic eggplant banchan that now makes a regular appearance at our dinner table.
- Selina

Prep Time / 10 min
Pressure Cook Time / 7 min
Release / Natural and Quick

3 Korean eggplants, cut into ½-inch baton pieces
1 Korean red chili pepper, diced
2 scallions, chopped
1 tbsp soy sauce
1 tsp guk ganjang (soup soy sauce)
1 tbsp white granulated sugar
1 tbsp gochugaru
1 tsp minced garlic
¼ tsp fine sea salt
2 tsp perilla oil
2 tsp roasted sesame seeds

1 Pour 2 cups of water into the inner pot and place a steamer basket inside. Place eggplant in the steamer basket.

2 Turn and lock the lid and move the steam release valve to the sealed position. Select Steam and program for 5 minutes. When the cooking is complete, allow the pressure to release naturally for 2 minutes, then quick-release any remaining pressure. Unlock and carefully remove the lid.

3 Sprinkle sea salt over the eggplant in the pot. Keep the lid off and let the eggplant cool.

4 In a large bowl, add chili pepper, scallions, soy sauce, guk ganjang, sugar, gochugaru, minced garlic, and sea salt and mix well.

5 Using tongs, transfer the eggplant into the bowl with seasonings. Once cool enough to touch, gently mix everything together by hand.

6 Drizzle perilla oil and garnish with roasted sesame seeds, then serve.

Tip Korean or Asian eggplants are lighter in color, longer, and thinner than globe eggplants. Eggplant should be firm to the touch and can be found at Asian grocers or farmers' markets.

gamja salad 감자 샐러드

korean-style potato salad

Serves 4

My mom never made gamja salad at home, so I was the first to dive into it when I'd spot it from the sea of banchan dishes at restaurants. The different variations of it include as few or many vegetables, and apples for a sweet balance. I add everything in mine because I love all the different crunchy textures and flavors against the creamy potato-y-ness. - *Nancy*

Prep Time / 25 min
Pressure Cook Time / 5 min
Release / Quick

1 Persian cucumber, deseeded, and cut into ¼-inch pieces

1 lb russet potatoes, peeled and cut into 1-inch chunks

2 large eggs

1 medium carrot, peeled and minced

½ cup canned corn, drained (optional)

1 small honeycrisp apple, peeled, and diced

½ cup mayonnaise

1 ½ tsp white granulated sugar

1 tsp, plus pinch kosher salt

1 tsp rice vinegar

Pinch ground black or white pepper

1 In a small bowl, add the cucumber and sprinkle with a pinch of kosher salt. Mix together and set aside.

2 Pour 1 cup of water into the inner pot and place a steamer basket inside. Place potatoes in the steamer basket. Layer the eggs on top.

3 Turn and lock the lid and move the steam release valve to the sealed position. Select Pressure Cook on High and program for 5 minutes.

4 In a medium bowl, prepare an ice bath with cold water and ice.

5 When the cooking is complete, quick-release manually. Unlock and carefully remove the lid.

6 Immediately transfer the eggs to the ice bath. Transfer the potatoes to a large bowl. Smash potatoes with a potato masher or a fork. The texture will get creamier as other ingredients are added.

7 Peel the eggs and dice the egg whites. Add to the mashed potato. Set the yolks aside for garnish.

8 Squeeze the excess liquid from the cucumber by hand. Add the cucumber, carrot, corn (if using), apple, mayonnaise, sugar, salt, vinegar, and a pinch of ground pepper to the mashed potato and mix together until combined. Season with more salt and pepper to taste.

9 Garnish individual servings with crumbled egg yolks. Serve chilled or at room temperature.

Tip Make sandwiches with any leftovers.

kong ja ban 콩자반

soy-braised black beans

Makes 2 cups

The little black soybeans in this dish are salty, sweet, and nutty. When the cooked beans cool, they firm up and get chewier in texture. As a kid, it was fun to eat this dish: one bean at a time. Carefully balanced between my chopsticks, I would try to get a single kernel to travel into my mouth, without slipping. I may have been showing off my chopsticks skills and channeling Mr. Miyagi from the movie, *Karate Kid*. It totally annoyed my parents. - *Nancy*

Prep Time / 5 min
Pressure Cook Time / 13 min
Release / Natural

1 cup seoritae (black soy beans with green kernels), rinsed and drained

3 tbsp soy sauce

2 tbsp white granulated sugar

2 tbsp oligodang (sweet syrup)

2 tbsp mirin

2 tbsp roasted sesame seeds

1 Place the beans into the inner pot. Add 1 cup of water.

2 Turn and lock the lid and move the steam release valve to the sealed position. Select Pressure Cook on the Bean setting and program for 13 minutes.

3 Stir together soy sauce, sugar, oligodang, and mirin in a small bowl.

4 When the cooking is complete, release the pressure naturally. Unlock and carefully remove the lid. Add the soy sauce mixture to the beans. Press the Sauté function on High and stir occasionally as the sauce begins to caramelize and thicken. Continuously stir the beans to avoid burning, about 8 minutes.

5 Turn off the Sauté function, stir in roasted sesame seeds, and immediately transfer to a bowl.

6 Allow to cool, then serve.

Tip Kong ja ban can be eaten cold or at room temperature. Store in an airtight container in the refrigerator for up to two weeks.

dubu jorim 두부조림

spicy seasoned tofu

Serves 4

Typically, tofu slices are pan-fried for this side dish. However, I prefer to make this version on days when I want to avoid oil splatters spraying me. When braised, the tofu texture becomes soft, resembling a thick stew. - *Nancy*

Prep Time / 10 min
Pressure Cook Time / 3 min
Release / Quick

1 (18 oz) block firm tofu

1 tbsp vegetable oil

½ medium onion, thinly sliced

2 large oyster mushrooms, cut in ¼-inch slices (optional)

3 tbsp soy sauce

1 tbsp minced garlic

2 tbsp gochugaru

1 tsp granulated white sugar

1 tsp kosher salt

1 Korean red chili pepper, thinly sliced (optional)

1 scallion, thinly sliced

1 tsp roasted sesame seeds

1 tbsp sesame oil

1 Cut the tofu block in half lengthwise and then cut evenly into ½-inch square slices. Set aside.

2 Select the Sauté function on High and add vegetable oil to the inner pot. When the oil is shimmering, add onions and mushrooms (if using). Sauté until the vegetables start to soften and edges brown, 2 to 3 minutes. Transfer to a bowl and set aside.

3 In a small bowl, mix together soy sauce, garlic, gochugaru, sugar, kosher salt, and 1 cup of water until well-combined.

4 Pour half of the sauce mixture into the inner pot, and place the tofu slices inside. Add the mushrooms and onions on top, pour the remaining sauce on top.

5 Turn and lock the lid in place with the steam release valve into the sealed position. Select Pressure Cook on High, program for 3 minutes. When the cooking is complete, quick-release pressure manually. Unlock and carefully remove the lid.

6 Select the Sauté function on High. Add the chili peppers (if using), scallion, sesame seeds, and drizzle in sesame oil. Cook on Sauté until the peppers soften and the sauce reduces, 2 to 3 minutes. Press Cancel.

7 Carefully remove the tofu into a serving bowl and ladle sauce on top.

Tip Caramelizing the onions and mushrooms adds more depth of flavor but for a faster version, skip Step 2 and add onions and mushrooms with the tofu at Step 4.

maneul jjong 마늘쫑

stir-fried garlic stems

Serves 4 to 6 (banchan servings)

This garlic stem banchan can be prepared in two ways: with a soy sauce base or a slightly spicy chili sauce base for seasoning. I like them both ways. Fresh garlic stems are seasonal and can be hard to come by. - *Selina*

Prep Time / 10 min
Cook Time / 10 min

1 lb garlic stems, trimmed, and cut into 2-inch pieces

1 tbsp cooking oil

18 garlic cloves (about 1 head of garlic)

2 tsp gochujang

1 tsp gochugaru

1 tbsp plum extract syrup

1 tbsp oligodang (sweet syrup)

1 tbsp sesame oil

1 tbsp roasted sesame seeds

1 In a medium pot over medium-high heat, bring 4 cups of water to boil. Add garlic stems to boil for about 4 to 5 minutes. Using a strainer, rinse, and drain the cooked garlic stems. Set aside.

2 On a heated frying pan, add the cooking oil. Then add garlic and garlic stems. Sauté on medium-high heat until dry but not browned, about 5 minutes. Let it cool.

3 In a medium bowl, whisk gochujang, gochugaru, plum extract syrup, oligodang, and sesame oil until well-combined. Add sautéed garlic and garlic stems. Toss together.

4 Sprinkle roasted sesame seeds to garnish and serve.

Tips

- As the stems absorb the seasoning, this dish will taste better after 3 to 5 days in the refrigerator.

- If using packaged garlic stems, skip Step 1. Soak in water and refrigerate overnight before adding the seasoning (they are super salty).

2

rice & noodles

Kongnamul Bap, page 42

kongnamul bap
콩나물밥
soybean sprout rice bowl
42

yung yang bap
영양밥
root veggie rice
43

jjajangmyeon
짜장면
black bean sauce noodles
45

japchae
잡채
stir-fry glass noodles
46

gondre mu bap
곤드레 무밥
korean thistle and radish rice
47

janchi guksu
잔치국수
wheat noodles in anchovies broth
48

yachae jook
야채죽
vegetable rice porridge
49

jun bok jook
전복죽
abalone porridge
50

tteokguk
떡국
rice cake soup
53

hobac jook
호박죽
pumpkin porridge
55

kongguksu
콩국수
soybean broth with noodles
57

rice
밥
instant pot rice
59

kongnamul bap 콩나물밥

soybean sprout rice bowl

Serves 4

Kongnamul bap is one of my family's favorite weekday meals. It is versatile and incredibly easy to make. When I'm in a rush, I tend to skip the seasoned beef and go with a fried egg instead. For a vegetarian version, substitute the meat with mushrooms. If I have leftover chili peppers and cilantro (yes, cilantro!), I mix it into my sauce and slather it in my rice bowl. - *Nancy*

Prep Time / 20 min

Pressure Cook Time / 3 min

Release / Natural and Quick

½ to ¾ lb soybean sprouts

2 cups short grain rice, rinsed and drained

2 tsp cooking oil

4 large eggs, fried (optional)

SEASONED BEEF (Optional)

½ lb ground beef, or thinly sliced steak

1 ½ tbsp soy sauce

1 tbsp mirin

2 tsp sesame oil

1 tsp minced garlic

Pinch of ground black pepper

SAUCE

¼ cup soy sauce

1 tsp white granulated sugar (optional)

1 tsp gochugaru

1 tsp roasted sesame seeds

2 tsp minced garlic

2 tsp sesame oil

2 scallions, thinly sliced

1 Combine all the ingredients for the seasoned beef (if using) in a bowl and set aside.

2 Fill a large bowl with cold water and add soybean sprouts. Discard floating soybean skins and shells and remove sprouts that have rotted or browned. Rinse and drain well.

3 Portion ¼ of the soybean sprouts into the inner pot and lay the rice on top. Add the remaining sprouts and 1 ¾ cups of water. Make sure the water covers the rice.

4 Turn and lock the lid and move the steam release valve to the sealed position. Select Pressure Cook on High and program for 3 minutes. Leave the Keep Warm function off. When the cooking is complete, release pressure naturally for 10 minutes, then quick-release any remaining pressure. Unlock and carefully remove the lid.

5 Gently mix the rice to combine, making sure not to smash any rice kernels. Let sit for about 2 minutes.

6 Heat a medium pan to medium-high heat, then add the cooking oil. Add seasoned beef marinade (if using) and cook until the meat is browned and no longer pink. Set aside.

7 In a small bowl, combine all the sauce ingredients together and set aside.

8 Divide the rice and soybean sprouts into individual serving bowls and top with beef or fried egg (if using). Serve with sauce and mix everything together to eat.

Tip To prevent sticking, spread a thin layer of cooking oil to the inner pot before cooking.

yung yang bap 영양밥

root veggie rice

Serves 4

Yung yang bap translates to nutritious rice. In Korea, you may find yung yang bap filled with fresh seafood, like oysters, seaweed, and other bountiful ingredients. Add wholesome ingredients to plain rice to bulk up with nutrition. I like to make my nutritious rice with root vegetables, for the extra vitamins and minerals. The extra fiber adds to a healthy daily diet and the Instant Pot does a fantastic job of making the rice super aromatic and flavorful. - *Selina*

Prep Time / 20 min
Pressure Cook Time / 3 min
Release / Natural and Quick

- **1 cup short-grain white rice, rinsed and drained**
- **½ cup sweet brown rice, rinsed and drained**
- **½ cup sweet white rice, rinsed and drained**
- **⅓ lotus root, sliced and cut into quarters**
- **½ burdock log, peeled and thinly julienned (see Tip)**
- **1 small carrot, peeled and thinly julienned (see Tip)**
- **1 cup gondre namul (Korean thistle), rinsed, drained, and trimmed**
- **4 roasted chestnuts, peeled and cut into quarters**

1 In a large bowl, combine white rice and brown and white sweet rice, and set aside.

2 Place the lotus root, burdock, carrot, gondre, and chestnuts to the bottom of the inner pot. Add the rice and 1½ cups of water. Turn and lock the lid and move the steam release valve to the sealed position. Select Pressure Cook on High and program for 3 minutes.

3 When the cooking is complete, release pressure naturally for 10 minutes, then quick-release any remaining pressure. Unlock and carefully remove the lid. Mix the rice and serve with Yangnyeom Ganjang (page 154).

Tips

- For ease, you can julienne the burdock and carrot using a mandolin or a slice peeler for vegetables.

- To save prep time, purchase precut ingredients found in the produce aisle (e.g., sliced lotus roots).

- Gondre namul can be found in the dried vegetable aisle at Korean markets. Replace gondre with any dried green vegetables of choice.

jjajangmyeon 짜장면

black bean sauce noodles

Serves 4 to 5

When I know I will be eating jjajangmyeon, I always make sure to wear dark clothing since black bean sauce tends to spatter everywhere when slurping noodles. Sometimes, I'll find little spots on my face and think I'd discovered a new mole or freckle, only to realize it was sauce speckles. - *Nancy*

Prep Time / 20 min
Pressure Cook Time / 3 min
Release / Quick

1 tbsp vegetable oil

½ lb pork shoulder, cut into small bite-sized pieces

1 cup chunjang (black bean sauce)

1 medium onion, diced

1 zucchini, cut into ½-inch dices

1 large Yukon Gold potato, peeled and cut into ½-inch cubes

2 tsp white granulated sugar

2 tbsp cornstarch

4 to 5 servings of jjajangmyeon noodles, or udon

½ English cucumber, deseeded and julienned (optional)

1 Preheat Instant Pot, set Sauté function on High and add 1 tablespoon of vegetable oil. When the oil is shimmering, add pork and sauté until the pork is browned.

2 Push the pork to one side of the pot and add chunjang to the other side. Stirring quickly, sauté the paste for about 1 minute to cook through.

3 Add the onion, zucchini, and potato to the pot and stir all the ingredients together to evenly coat with sauce. Stir in sugar and 3 cups of water.

4 Turn and lock the lid and move the steam release valve to the sealed position. Select Pressure Cook on High and program for 3 minutes. When the cooking is complete, quick-release pressure manually and press Cancel.

5 Unlock and carefully remove the lid and press Sauté on High. In a small bowl, mix cornstarch and ¼ cup of water together. Stir in the slurry to the sauce and cook until the sauce has thickened, about 2 to 3 minutes. Add sugar or salt to taste. Press Cancel.

6 Bring a large pot of water to boil. Cook the jjajangmyeon noodles according to the package's instructions. Drain and rinse the jjajangmyeon noodles. Divide the jjajangmyeon noodles into individual serving bowls.

7 Ladle sauce over serving bowls of jjajangmyeon noodles. Garnish with cucumbers (if using) and serve.

Tip For jjajangbap, try the sauce over rice. Serve with a side of kimchi or danmuji (Korean pickled radish). For jjajangmyeon noodles or udon substitute, use spaghetti noodles.

japchae 잡채

stir-fry glass noodles

Serves 4 (side dish), or serves 2 (main)

I really can't get over how convenient it is to make japchae in the Instant Pot. This vegetarian version is so easy, fast, and delicious. My mom always complained about how time consuming it was to make japchae: Stir fry each individual ingredient, cook the noodles, stir fry the noodles, then mix the cooked ingredients together with the sauce, phew! If I told her this version only takes about 20 minutes, her head would explode. To be fair, mine did too! - Nancy

Prep Time / 15 min
Pressure Cook Time / 3 min
Release / Quick

4 servings dangmyeon (sweet potato starch noodle)

1 carrot, peeled and julienned

½ onion, cut into ¼-inch slices

2 cups oyster mushrooms, cut into bite-sized pieces

1 ½ tbsp white granulated sugar

3 tbsp soy sauce

2 tsp vegetable oil

2 cups baby spinach

1 scallion, thinly sliced

1 tbsp sesame oil

Pinch of black pepper (optional)

1 tsp roasted sesame seeds (optional)

1 If dangmyeon noodles are long, carefully cut the noodles with scissors to fit the diameter of the inner pot. Lay the noodles in a criss-cross pattern to prevent clumping.

2 Lay the carrots, onions, and mushrooms on top of the noodles.

3 In a small bowl, whisk sugar, soy sauce, vegetable oil, and ¾ cup of water until well-combined. Drizzle the liquid mixture over the vegetables and noodles.

4 Turn and lock the lid and move the steam release valve to the sealed position. Select Pressure Cook on High and program for 3 minutes. When the cooking is complete, quick-release pressure manually and press Cancel. Unlock and carefully remove the lid.

5 Select Sauté on Low. Add ¼ cup water, baby spinach, scallion, sesame oil, and black pepper. Mix thoroughly with the noodles. If the noodles are clumped together, add water, 1 tablespoon at a time, to loosen it up. Keep sautéing ingredients together until the baby spinach has wilted and water is absorbed, about 2 to 3 minutes. Press Cancel.

6 Transfer japchae to a bowl. Garnish with roasted sesame seeds and serve.

Tip If possible, purchase 7- to 8-inch straight dangmyeon noodles for ease and convenience.

gondre mu bap 곤드레 무밥

korean thistle & radish rice

Serves 2 to 3

I've recently rekindled my relationship with Korean dried wild greens. I thought these vegetables and herbs were reserved only for special occasions, like Jungwol Daeboreum (first full moon of the lunar new year), but learned they are ordinary ingredients and consumed throughout the Korean peninsula. More commonly eaten outside of the city, wild greens are an essential part of daily meals in Korean Buddhist temples, where plants grow freely near the mountains. From the same aster plant family as chwinamul, gondre (Korean thistle) has aromatic and earthy flavors that match wonderfully with rice and Doenjang Jjigae (page 78). - *Selina*

Prep Time / 5 min, plus 30 min to soak

Pressure Cook Time / 5 min

Release / Natural and Quick

1 cup dried gondre (Korean thistle)
1 cup white rice, rinsed and drained
1 cup brown rice, rinsed and drained
¼ small mu (Korean radish), or daikon, peeled and shredded

1 In a medium bowl, cover gondre in water, and soak, about 30 minutes to 1 hour. Drain and rinse. With scissors, roughly cut the leaves into bite-sized pieces and trim stems that are tough.

2 In the inner pot, add the white and brown rice, and 1 cup of water. Stir to combine and level the rice evenly. Add gondre and mu on top.

3 Turn and lock the lid and move the steam release valve to the sealed position. Select Pressure Cook on High and program for 5 minutes. When the cooking is compete, release pressure naturally for 10 minutes, then quick-release any remaining pressure. Unlock and carefully remove the lid.

4 Serve with Yangnyeom Ganjang (page 154).

Tip For fluffy and firm rice kernels, keep the rice in Keep Warm mode for an additional 5 minutes with the glass lid before serving.

janchi guksu 잔치국수

wheat noodles in anchovy broth

Serves 4 to 5

This noodle soup is one of my mom's favorite dishes. The anchovies in the broth add depth to the flavors, and the toppings bring layers of refreshing brightness. When I made this recipe for her, she gave me her two thumbs up. I was pretty darn pleased with myself. In my opinion, kimchi is a must-have with this dish, but you do you. Freeze and use leftover broth for other soups and stews. - *Nancy*

Prep Time / 25 min
Pressure Cook Time / 20 min
Release / Natural and Quick

1 cup medium to large myeolchi (dried anchovies), heads and guts removed

1 small yellow onion, halved

½ lb mu (Korean radish), or daikon, peeled and cut into large chunks

3 scallions, halved

2 pieces dashima (dried kelp), cut into 3-inch squares

3 dried shiitake mushrooms, soaked and sliced (optional)

1 tsp cooking oil

1 zucchini, julienned

1 large carrot, julienned

1 cup baby bella mushrooms, sliced

4 to 5 servings somyeon (wheat flour noodles)

Egg Jidan (Egg Crepe Garnish, see page 74)

1 Select Sauté on High and add myeolchi to the inner pot. Do not add any oil and toast the myeolchi, about 5 to 8 minutes.

2 Add onion, mu, scallions, dashima, dried shiitake mushrooms (if using), and 11 cups of water to the pot.

3 Turn and lock the lid and move the steam release valve to the sealed position. Select Pressure Cook on High and program for 20 minutes.

4 Heat a non-stick frying pan over medium-high heat. Add cooking oil and sauté the zucchini, about 1 to 2 minutes. Season with salt and pepper. Transfer to a large plate. Repeat with julienned carrots.

5 In the same pan, sauté the mushroom until soft and browned, about 2 to 3 minutes. Season with salt and pepper. Transfer to the plate.

6 Bring a large pot of water to boil over medium high heat. Add somyeon and cook according to the package's instructions. Drain noodles in a large strainer and rinse thoroughly in cold water. Drain and divide into serving bowls.

7 When the cooking is complete, release pressure naturally for 20 minutes, then quick-release any remaining pressure. Unlock and carefully remove the lid. Pour the broth through a strainer and add salt to taste.

8 Arrange the toppings and egg jidan neatly on top of the noodles and ladle anchovy broth into serving bowls. Serve immediately.

yachae jook 야채죽

vegetable rice porridge

Serves 4 to 5

I crave this dish every time I get sick. It's easy on the tummy, warm, and satisfying. If food could be a hug, it would be jook. Swap out the listed veggies and use broccoli, celery, or spinach. Adding salt to the pot of jook can change the consistency, so season individual serving bowls with salt to taste. I always start with a little drizzle of sesame oil, soy sauce, and a small sprinkle of salt and pepper in my bowl. - *Nancy*

Prep Time / 25 min
Pressure Cook Time / 20 min
Release / Natural and Quick

1 ½ tbsp vegetable oil

2 tsp minced garlic

1 cup minced onion

1 cup minced shiitake mushrooms

1 cup minced zucchini

1 carrot, peeled and minced

1 cup white rice (short or medium grain), rinsed and drained

TOPPINGS (Optional)

1 scallion, thinly sliced

Roasted sesame seeds

Roasted gim (seasoned seaweed laver) cut into strips

SEASONINGS (Optional)

Guk ganjang (soup soy sauce) or regular soy sauce

Sesame oil

Salt

Pepper

1 Select Sauté on Low and add vegetable oil to the inner pot. When the oil is shimmering, add garlic and onions. Sauté until onions are soft. Add mushrooms, zucchini, carrot, and rice. Stir and sauté the ingredients, about 2 minutes.

2 In the inner pot, add rice and 5 cups of water (or for thinner jook, add 6 cups) and stir well.

3 Turn and lock the lid and move the steam release valve to the sealed position. Select the Porridge setting on Low, and program for 20 minutes. When the cooking is complete, release pressure naturally for 10 minutes., then quick-release any remaining pressure. Unlock and carefully remove the lid.

4 Stir jook and divide into individual serving bowls. Top with toppings of choice and serve with seasonings on the side.

Tip For a thinner jook, stir in warm water until preferred consistency is achieved before serving.

jun bok jook 전복죽

abalone porridge

Serves 4 to 6

Jun bok jook is one of my favorite porridges. When I was growing up, my mom made different types of jook—jun bok (abalone) and ahwook (curled mallow) were two of my favorites. I don't recall abalone innards in my mom's original jook, she may have thought it wouldn't be palatable for my developing taste buds. When abalone innards are added to jook, it will turn green and have an extra earthy, sea-like flavor. I recently made this for my mom while she was recovering from surgery. The care and love put into cooking for loved ones have healing powers and jun bok jook is definitely a special dish for me. - *Selina*

Prep Time / 30 min
Pressure Cook Time / 20 min
Release / Quick

6 (9.2 oz pack) small to medium frozen abalone

2 tsp sesame oil , plus more for garnish

¼ cup onion, chopped

1 tsp minced garlic

2 cups short-grain white rice, rinsed and drained

½ tbsp unsalted butter

Pinch of sea salt

Jook sauce (optional, page 156)

Special equipment: small kitchen brush or toothbrush

1 Thaw and clean the abalone. (see "How to Clean Abalone" on the following page). Diagonally cut the meat of abalone into thin slices. In a small bowl, set aside some abalone slices for the garnish.

2 Select Sauté on Low and add sesame oil. Add onion, garlic, and sauté until onion becomes translucent. Add the abalone gut innards (if using), and sauté until lightly browned and dry, about 2 to 3 minutes. Add the rice and abalone, and sauté for 1 minute. Add 8 cups of water. Do not let the ingredients stick to the bottom of the pot. Press Cancel.

3 Turn and lock the lid and move the steam release valve to the sealed position. Select Porridge on High and program for 20 minutes.

4 While jook is cooking, heat a pan over medium-low heat with butter and a pinch of sea salt. Sauté the abalone garnish, about 1 to 2 minutes. Set aside.

5 When the cooking is complete, quick-release pressure manually. Unlock and carefully remove the lid. On the Keep Warm setting, slowly add 1 cup of water at a time and stir until achieving desired porridge consistency. For a thinner porridge, add up to 3 to 4 cups of water. Season with salt to taste or add Jook sauce (page 156).

(recipe continues)

jun bok jook

전복죽

abalone porridge
(continued)

6 Top with sautéed abalone, drizzle sesame oil on top, and serve.

Tip For a more savory and plain jook, omit the abalone innards. If using abalone innards, cook thoroughly with onion and garlic before adding water at Step 2 to remove any unwanted flavors and smells.

how to clean abalone

Soak thawed abalone in cold water.

Using a small brush like a toothbrush, clean around the shell body on the sides and tops (A).

Gently insert a metal spoon into the bottom rounded part of the shell to shuck the meat (B). Innards should still be attached. With a knife, cut the innards from the body (C). Blue innards are male, yellow innards are female but no different in taste.

Pull and remove the tooth (the white hard pointy part of the meat) using a knife, or scissor to detach the entire area (D). Place the innards in a small bowl and cut into small bite-sized pieces (E).

Clean the abalone meat in running water and brush off any remaining dirt. Diagonally cut into thin slices to produce longer pieces (F). Abalone will reduce in size when cooked.

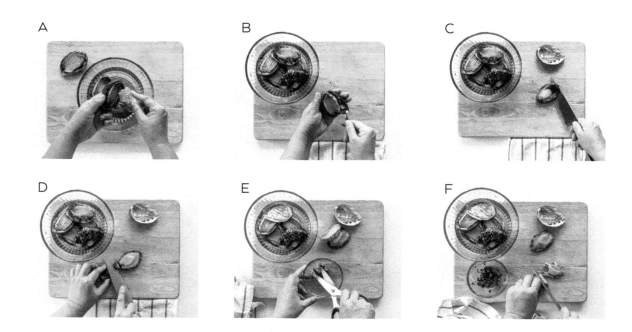

tteokguk 떡국

rice cake soup

Serves 4

When I was little, I wondered why my family celebrated New Year's Day twice a year. We'd gather with extended family on January 1 and about one month later, we'd have another celebration. The gatherings entailed eating tteokguk, saebae (traditional bowing to elders for words of wisdom and money for an auspicious new year), and playing folk games like yutnori—all while wearing hanbok (traditional Korean wear). I realized later my father's side celebrated according to the western calendar on January 1 and my mother's side, based on the lunar calendar on Gujeong or Seollal. They say you become a year older and wiser after eating a bowl of tteokguk on New Year's. I've had two bowls of tteokguk every New Year's Day, so that makes me about 100 years old now! - *Selina*

Prep Time / 5 min
Pressure Cook Time / 10 min
Release / Quick

1 lb tteokguk tteok (coin-shaped sliced rice cakes)

½ lb top sirloin steak

2 large eggs

½ onion, peeled and cut

4 garlic cloves

2 scallions, stems and roots, plus thin slices for garnish

1 ½ tsp fine sea salt

¼ tsp ground black pepper

¼ cup gim jaban (toasted seaweed flakes)

1 If using frozen tteokguk tteok, soak in a bowl of cold water and set aside, about 15 to 20 minutes. Rinse the steak in cold running water to remove blood.

2 In a small bowl, whisk two eggs together and set aside.

3 In the inner pot, add steak (whole), onion, garlic, scallion stems and roots, and 6 cups of water.

4 Turn and lock the lid and move the steam release valve to the sealed position. Select Pressure Cook on High and program for 10 minutes. When the cooking is complete, quick-release pressure manually. Unlock and carefully remove the lid.

5 Remove and discard the aromatics and transfer the steak to a plate. Once the beef is cool enough to touch, cut into bite-sized pieces.

6 Select Sauté on Low. Once the broth simmers, add tteok slices, steak, and whisked egg. Stir and bring to boil, about 5 minutes. Season with salt and pepper. When the tteok slices float to the surface, they are cooked through and ready to eat.

7 Serve tteokguk in individual bowls. Garnish with sliced scallions and gim jaban.

hobac jook 호박죽

pumpkin porridge

Serves 5 to 6

Warm and satisfying, hobac jook is the perfect comfort food for a cold winter day. The salt and sugar measurements are listed as a starting point, so depending on preference, add more salt or sugar to taste. Saealsim add a nice chewy texture and are so easy to make.
- *Nancy*

Prep Time / 30 min

Pressure Cook Time / 20 min

Release / Quick

1 medium kabocha squash

¼ cup sweet rice flour (Mochiko)

½ tsp kosher salt

1 to 3 tbsp brown sugar (optional)

SAEALSIM 새알심 (Sweet Rice Balls)

½ cup sweet rice flour (Mochiko brand)

¼ tsp kosher salt

4 tbsp boiling hot water

TOPPINGS (Optional)

Red beans, cooked

Pine nuts

Roasted and shelled pumpkin seeds

Dried jujubes, deseeded and thinly sliced

Special equipment: Masher, immersion blender, or standard blender

1 Place a trivet inside the inner pot and put the whole kabocha squash on top. Pour 1 cup of water into the pot.

2 Turn and lock the lid and move the steam release valve to the sealed position. Select Pressure Cook on High and program for 5 minutes. When the cooking is complete, quick-release pressure manually.

3 Using oven mitts, carefully take out the squash and set on a cutting board. Remove the trivet from the inner pot and discard the water. Once the squash is cool enough to handle, cut in half. With a spoon, scoop out the seeds and stringy bits and shave off the skin with a knife.

4 Dice the squash into 1 ½-inch cubes and place into the inner pot. Add 3 cups of water or enough to just cover the squash.

5 Turn and lock the lid and move the steam release valve to the sealed position. Select Porridge on High and program for 15 minutes. When the cooking is complete, quick-release pressure manually and press Cancel. Unlock and carefully remove the lid.

6 Using a masher or an immersion blender, mash or blend the squash until smooth. Alternatively, use a blender to combine the squash and water together. Once smooth, transfer the squash mixture to the inner pot.

(recipe continues)

hobac jook

호박죽

pumpkin porridge
(continued)

7 In a small bowl, mix the sweet rice flour and ⅓ cup water to make a gooey paste. Slowly pour the slurry into the jook. While pouring, use a whisk to gently combine the slurry and jook together to avoid lumps.

8 Select Sauté on Low. Simmer until the jook has thickened, about 1 to 3 minutes. Stir often to prevent the jook from sticking or burning. When the jook has reached a thick consistency, press Cancel. Add salt and sugar (if using) to taste.

9 Transfer hobac jook to bowls and add your favorite toppings.

Tip Adding the sweet rice slurry may add lumps to the jook. For a more velvety jook, use an immersion blender to purée the porridge.

To make Saealsim (Sweet Rice Balls)

1 In a medium bowl, mix sweet rice flour and salt together. Add boiling water and with a spoon, mix the flour and water together. The dough will be crumbly at first, but keep working it together.

2 When the dough is cool enough to handle, knead the dough until it forms into a smooth ball.

3 Use sweet rice flour to lightly flour a flat surface. Roll the dough onto the flat surface into a thick string, about ½- to ¾-inch thick. Cut the dough into ½-inch pieces and place a damp towel over the dough.

4 Roll each piece into a ball. Place them under a damp towel to prevent drying.

5 Bring a medium pot of water to boil. When the water is boiling, add the rice balls. In a medium bowl, prepare an ice bath with cold water and ice.

6 When the rice balls float to the surface, use a slotted spoon to scoop out and transfer to the cold water bath. Set aside. Add rice balls to jook before serving.

kongguksu 콩국수

soybean broth with noodles

Serves 4

Everyone in the house knew when Mom was making kongguksu because our old Osterizer blender would be going full blast for what seemed like forever. It was worth all the noise though, especially on hot summer days. The cold soybean milk broth is light and nutty, and pairs perfectly with somyeon. While the Instant Pot cuts down on hours and hours of soaking time, the broth tends to have a pale yellow color from the beans, while traditional kongguksu is more white in color. If you've forgotten to soak your beans overnight (as I often do), don't worry. This version is still incredibly refreshing and delicious. - *Nancy*

Prep Time / 15 min, plus
  soaking time
Pressure Cook Time / 20 min
Release / Natural

1 cup meju kong (dried soybeans)

4 servings of somyeon (wheat flour noodles)

1 tbsp roasted sesame seeds, plus more for garnish

½ English cucumber, julienned

4 hard-boiled eggs (optional, page 31), cut into halves

Special equipment: Blender

1 Wash and soak dried meju kong in a bowl of water for 1 hour.

2 Rinse the meju kong thoroughly and discard any bean skins and shells that have come off. Drain well and place meju kong in the inner pot. Add 4 cups of water to the pot and close the lid.

3 Turn and lock the lid and move the steam release valve to the sealed position. Select Pressure Cook on High and program for 20 minutes. Leave the Keep Warm function off.

4 Bring a large pot of water to boil over medium-high heat. Add somyeon and cook according to the package's instructions. Drain noodles in a large strainer and rinse thoroughly in cold running water. Drain and set aside.

5 When the cooking is complete, release pressure naturally. Unlock and carefully remove the lid. Drain the water and rinse the meju kong in cold water. Using your hands, agitate the beans to release loose soybean skins. Add more water to the pot if needed and remove any floating skin. Using a strainer, drain to remove the meju kong.

(recipe continues)

kongguksu

콩국수

soybean broth with noodles
(continued)

6 In a blender, add the cooked meju kong, roasted sesame seeds, and 2 ½ cups cold water. Purée until very smooth and creamy. For a thinner consistency, add about ¼ cup of water and blend again. (Keep adding water, ¼ cup at a time, until desired consistency is reached.)

7 Transfer the meju kong milk broth to an airtight container and refrigerate to chill. To serve immediately, add ice cubes to serving bowls to chill the broth.

8 To serve, divide the noodles into individual serving bowls. Give the meju kong milk broth a good stir and pour over the noodles. Garnish with cucumbers, roasted sesame seeds, and hard boiled eggs (if using). Serve with salt on the side.

Tips

- For a smoother and milkier broth, pour the meju kong milk broth through a fine mesh strainer after blending.

- Add salt to individual bowls when ready to eat and serve. Adding salt before storing can spoil the meju kong milk broth.

- Leftover meju kong milk broth can be stored in an airtight container for up to 3 to 4 days in the refrigerator.

- For a more nutty flavor, add 2 tablespoons of roasted peanuts, pine nuts, walnuts, almonds, or even peanut butter with meju kong before blending together at Step 6.

rice 밥

instant pot rice

Serves 4

Making perfect rice isn't as easy as it seems. There are different methods to make rice: using rice cookers, cast iron pots, clay pots, stoneware pots and I was determined to find a way to make the perfect rice in the Instant Pot. While the Instant Pot operates differently than standard rice cookers, this version makes an even, soft and fluffy rice that doesn't stick to the bottom. Make sure to give it a try! - *Selina*

Prep Time / 2 min
Pressure Cook Time / 3 min
Release / Natural and Quick

2 cups medium-grain white rice (sushi rice), or brown rice, rinsed and drained

2 cups water

1 In the inner pot, add rice and 2 cups of water (1:1 ratio). Make sure the rice is evenly distributed across the bottom of the pot.

2 Turn and lock the lid and move the steam release valve to the sealed position. Select Pressure Cook on High and program for 3 minutes. When the cooking is complete, release naturally for 10 minutes, then quick-release any remaining pressure. Unlock and carefully remove the lid.

Tip For a more textured rice, use less water (1:¾ cup rice to water ratio). For brown rice or mixed grain rice (i.e., purple rice), use 1:1 ratio.

3
soups & stews

Kimchi Jjigae, page 62

kimchi jjigae
김치찌개
kimchi stew
62

soondubu jjigae
순두부찌개
silken tofu stew
63

yukgaejang
육개장
spicy beef soup
64

sagol gomtang
사골곰탕
beef bone soup
67

kkori gomtang
꼬리곰탕
oxtail soup
69

gamjatang
감자탕
pork bone soup
70

galbitang
갈비탕
beef short rib soup
73

miyeok guk
미역국
seaweed soup
75

sogogi muguk
소고기 무국
beef radish soup
76

baechu guk
배추국
cabbage soup
77

doenjang jjigae
된장찌개
soybean paste stew
78

budae jjigae
부대찌개
korean army stew
81

gochujang jjigae
고추장찌개
chili pepper paste stew
82

kongbiji jjigae
콩비지 찌개
ground soybean stew
83

kimchi jjigae 김치찌개

kimchi stew

Serves 4 to 6

This is the ultimate Korean comfort food. When the kimchi in your fridge starts to age and becomes a little fizzy, it is time to make kimchi jjigae. The flavor profile runs deep and so much hotness. Amp up the spice by adding more gochujang. In our household, my dad, sister, and I were such dubu (tofu) hoarders that my mother would have to use two packs to satiate our dubu needs. If you are also a dubu hoarder, please, use the entire pack for this fiery stew. - *Nancy*

Prep Time / 20 min

Pressure Cook Time / 10 min

Release / Quick

1 tbsp vegetable oil

½ lb pork shoulder or pork belly, cut into bite-sized pieces

1 small onion, thinly sliced

3 ½ cups kimchi

2 garlic cloves, minced

½ cup kimchi juice

2 tbsp gochujang

½ to 1 tsp white granulated sugar*

½ tsp kosher salt

3 cups stock (see Tip)

1 tbsp soy sauce

1 (12 oz) block regular or firm tofu, cut lengthwise and then cut into ½-inch slices

1 tsp sesame oil

2 scallions, thinly sliced

* Taste your kimchi! Sugar can help neutralize sour kimchi flavors. If the kimchi is on the sweeter side, use little to no sugar. If the kimchi has no sweetness, add sugar. Adjust later to taste as needed.

1 Add the vegetable oil to the inner pot and select the Sauté function. When the oil is shimmering, add pork and onion. Sauté until the pork is nearly cooked and the onion is tender, about 3 minutes.

2 Add kimchi and garlic to the pot and sauté for 4 to 5 minutes. Then add kimchi juice, gochujang, and stir until combined. Next, add sugar, kosher salt, stock, and soy sauce.

3 Turn and lock the lid and move the steam release valve to the sealed position. Select Pressure Cook on High and program for 10 minutes. When the cooking is complete, quick-release manually. Unlock and carefully remove the lid.

4 Select Sauté on High and add tofu. Ladle some broth over the tofu as it simmers and cook until the tofu is heated through, about 2 to 3 minutes.

5 Drizzle in sesame oil and mix gently. Taste and add salt if needed. Add scallions.

6 Transfer stew in serving bowls and serve with rice.

Tips

- For the base, use water, rice water (see Glossary, page 165) or preferred stock, like Man Neung Myeolchi Yooksu (page 139).

- For a vegetarian version, omit the pork and use shiitake mushrooms. Use either kelp broth, water, or rice water for the stock.

soondubu jjigae 순두부찌개

silken tofu stew

Serves 4 to 6

When a friend told me he didn't like tofu, we promptly went to my favorite soondubu jjigae restaurant. When the bubbling stews arrived in earthenware bowls, I told him now was the time to crack a raw egg and stir it in. The silky tofu with spicy, boiling hot broth won him over. Instead of individual bowls, this recipe makes one big pot of stew. Add eggs in at the end if you want to use them. - *Nancy*

Prep Time / 15 min
Pressure Cook Time / 5 min
Release / Quick

4 tbsp gochugaru

2 tbsp fish sauce

2 tbsp soy sauce

½ tsp kosher salt

2 tsp minced garlic

2 tbsp sesame oil

½ lb ground pork

1 medium yellow onion, peeled and diced

1 anchovy dry stock pack (see Tip)

1 zucchini, diced into ½-inch pieces

1 ½ cups diced mushrooms (shiitake, crimini, bunapi, or mix)

2 (16-oz) block silken tofu

3 large eggs

3 scallions, thinly sliced

1 In a small bowl make the soondubu paste by mixing gochugaru, fish sauce, soy sauce, kosher salt, and garlic together. Set aside.

2 Select Sauté on High and add sesame oil. Add pork, onion, and the soondubu paste. Sauté and stir together until the pork is cooked and onions become translucent. Press Cancel and add 3 ½ cups water, anchovy stock pack, zucchini, and mushrooms.

3 Turn and lock the lid and move the steam release valve to the sealed position. Select Pressure Cook on High and program for 5 minutes. When the cooking is complete, quick-release pressure manually. Unlock and carefully remove the lid. Discard the anchovy stock pack.

4 Select Sauté on High. Add silken tofu in large chunks. When the soup comes to a boil, crack and add eggs and gently stir. Cook for about 3 to 5 minutes or until the eggs have cooked to preferred doneness. Add salt to taste.

5 Press Cancel and serve in individual bowls. Garnish with scallions and serve with a side of rice.

Tips

- For stock substitution, use 3 ½ cups of desired stock or water with 2 teaspoons of fish sauce.

- For a meatless version, omit pork and sauté onions and mushrooms with the soondubu paste instead.

yukgaejang 육개장

spicy beef soup

Serves 4

Yukgaejang, or spicy beef soup, was part of my grandmother's reper-
toire menu. Whenever she hosted big family gatherings, she would
make a huge pot of this soup. It was almost expected that she would
make it and everyone looked forward to eating it. My mom does the
same thing and I'm trying to continue their legacy. The shredded
beef and dae pa simmered in spicy broth makes a deep and rich flavor. When you add gosari, it adds a bit of woodsy flavor. - *Selina*

Prep Time / 15 min, plus 30 min
  to soak
Pressure Cook Time / 5 min
Release / Natural and Quick

1 lb brisket beef

1 medium onion, ½ for stock,
  ½ sliced

1 dae pa (Korean green onion), cut
  into 2-inch pieces (save roots
  for stock)

3 tbsp sesame oil

3 tbsp gochugaru

½ cup cooked gosari (fernbrake),
  rinsed then trimmed

½ cup mung bean sprouts, rinsed

½ cup oyster mushrooms, shredded
  by hand

1 tsp fine sea salt

1 tbsp minced garlic

2 tbsp guk ganjang (soup soy sauce)

1 Soak the brisket in a large bowl of cold water for
30 minutes to remove blood. In the inner pot, add beef,
onion half, and dae pa root with 6 cups of water.

2 Turn and lock the lid and move the steam release valve to
the sealed position. Select Pressure Cook on High and program for 5 minutes. When the cooking is complete, release
pressure naturally for about 5 minutes and quick-release any
remaining pressure. Unlock and carefully remove the lid.

3 Remove the aromatics. Transfer beef to a dish and using
two forks, shred the beef into strips. Transfer the broth to a
large bowl and rinse the inner pot with warm water.

4 Select Sauté on Low and add sesame oil and onion slices.
Sauté until the onions have softened, about 3 to 4 minutes.
Add gochugaru and sauté for another 2 minutes.

5 Select Sauté on High and add the beef stock, brisket
shreds, dae pa, gosari, mung bean sprouts, mushrooms, and
1 cup of water. When it comes to a high boil, stir in sea salt,
minced garlic, and guk ganjang to season. Let it continue to
boil and stir occasionally for about 5 minutes. Add more guk
ganjang or salt to taste.

6 Serve over a bowl of rice on the side.

Tip Try adding ingredients like egg and dangmyeon (sweet
potato starch noodle). Whisk 1 egg in a small bowl and soak
dangmyeon in warm water. Add to soup at Step 5 and
continue cooking on Sauté for 5 minutes.

sagol gomtang 사골곰탕

beef bone broth

Serves 4 to 6

There is a Korean joke about when Korean moms make a huge pot of sagol gomtang, she's preparing to run away! The soup's lifespan can be extended multiple times by boiling with water which can feed the family for days. But jokes aside, this is truly a comforting bone broth that families can enjoy. It also freezes well so this can serve as a base for other types of soups and stews. There are two important notes shared under Tips. I recommend using ox feet bones and boiling on high heat to create a thick milky broth. Check it out! - *Selina*

Prep Time / 1 hr to soak

Pressure Cook Time / 30 min, plus 45 min to boil

Release / Natural

3 to 4 lbs mixed beef bones (ox feet, shank, or knee bones)

1 lb flank steak or brisket

1 serving somyeon (wheat flour noodles)

1 scallion, thinly sliced

1 Wash and soak the bones in cold water for 1 hour draining and replacing the water every 20 minutes. Place the bones and brisket in the inner pot with 12 cups of water.

2 Turn and lock the lid and move the steam release valve to the sealed position. Select Pressure Cook on High and program for 30 minutes. When the cooking is complete, release pressure naturally. Unlock and carefully remove the lid.

3 Transfer the brisket and bones to a large bowl. Discard the water and rinse the bones clean under cold running water.

4 In the inner pot, add bones, brisket, and water up to the 3-quart line, about 10 to 12 cups. Select Sauté on High and boil for 45 minutes with the lid off. Keep adding water up to the 3-quart line as it continues to boil. Using a spoon and a skimmer, skim the fat and solids from the broth. Continue until the broth becomes clean and translucent.

5 Transfer bones and meat to a cutting board. Season the broth with salt and pepper. Slice the meat into thin slices and remove ligaments from the bones (it should fall apart easily).

(recipe continues)

sagol gomtang

사골곰탕

beef bone soup

(*continued*)

6 In a medium pot over medium-high heat, bring 4 cups of water to boil. Add somyeon and cook for 2 to 3 minutes, or according to the package's instructions. Thoroughly rinse and drain the noodles in cold running water.

7 Serve the broth and meat with rice and/or noodles (if using). Garnish with scallions and season with salt, as needed.

Tips

- Natural release may take time. Release pressure a little bit at a time to avoid liquid from overflowing. Ensure the liquid collector at the back of the Instant Pot is not full.

- For a milky bone broth, use ox feet with shank bones and boil on high starting Step 4.

- Store the bone broth in the freezer for later use.

- Store bones in the freezer and reuse up to 3 times. The second or third boil will produce a thicker and milkier bone broth.

kkori gomtang 꼬리곰탕

oxtail soup

Serves 5 to 6

The broth is simple but flavor-rich and the oxtail meat is incredibly tender and soft. Everyone seasons their bowls to their liking with salt, pepper, and scallions at the table. My mom always had a spicy paste on the side for those who wanted a spicier soup. Although it takes some time to make, this version saves some time and fuss. Let me tell you, that tender oxtail meat and broth is so worth it. - *Nancy*

Prep Time / 15 min, plus 1 hr to soak
Pressure Cook Time / 50 min
Release / Natural

3 lbs oxtail, excess fat trimmed

½ lb mu (Korean radish), peeled, halved lengthwise

4 garlic cloves, peeled and crushed

2 to 4 scallions, thinly sliced

SPICY PASTE

4 garlic cloves, minced

2 tbsp gochugaru

1 tbsp fish sauce

1 tsp kosher salt

1 tsp ground black pepper

1 Place oxtails in a large pot. Cover with cold water and soak for 1 hour, draining and replacing the water every 20 minutes. Transfer oxtails to the inner pot and add about 5 cups of water or enough to cover the oxtail.

2 Turn and lock the lid and move the steam release valve to the sealed position. Select Pressure Cook on High and program for 10 minutes. When the cooking is complete, quick-release pressure manually. Unlock and carefully remove the lid.

3 Drain and rinse the oxtails and clean the inner pot. Place oxtails, mu, and garlic cloves in the inner pot. Add water to reach just below the maximum PC fill line, about 5 cups.

4 Turn and lock the lid and move the steam release valve to the sealed position. Select Pressure Cook on High and program for 40 minutes. When the cooking is complete, release pressure naturally. Unlock and carefully remove the lid.

5 Transfer the oxtails, mu, and garlic to a bowl. Use a spoon and a skimmer to remove the fat and solids from the broth. If the radish chunks are very thick, cut into ¼-inch slices. Divide the radish and oxtail into serving bowls.

6 In a small bowl, add all spicy paste ingredients and mix.

7 Pour broth into bowls and serve with a side of rice. Serve with scallions, kosher salt, black pepper, and spicy paste on the side.

Tip Refrigerate the broth overnight after Step 7. The solidified fat can be easily skimmed the next day.

gamjatang 감자탕

pork bone soup

Serves 4 to 6

For the longest time, I thought this dish was called gamjatang because of the potatoes. Potato and the pork backbone are both known as gamja in Korean—and this dish calls for big potato chunks. Gamjatang has flavorful elements: wooguhji (boiled young napa cabbage), kkaennip, and deulkkae garu. But the deep milky broth from simmering the bones and the tender pork are the real highlights. Restaurants specialize in this dish, but now I can make it from the comfort of my home with the Instant Pot. - *Selina*

Prep Time / 10 min, plus 1 hr to soak

Pressure Cook Time / 15 min

Release / Natural

4 lbs pork backbone (with meat)

1 small onion, cut in half

4 scallions, stems and roots

1 (1 ½-inch) piece ginger, peeled and thinly sliced

6 garlic cloves

2 tbsp soju or mirin

2 to 4 whole young napa cabbage

1 tsp fine sea salt

4 small yellow potatoes

4 kkaennip (perilla) or shiso leaves, shredded

deulkkae garu (perilla powder), to taste (optional)

¼ cup scallions, thinly sliced (green parts)

SEASONING

1 tbsp doenjang

1 tbsp gochujang

2 tbsp gochugaru

2 tbsp soy sauce

2 tbsp garlic, minced

1 tsp fine sea salt

1 In a large pot or bowl, soak the pork bones in cold water for 1 hour, draining and replacing the water every 20 minutes.

2 In a small mixing bowl, combine the seasoning ingredients and set aside.

3 Select Sauté on High and add the pork, onion, scallion stems and roots, ginger, garlic cloves, and soju with 8 cups of water. Bring to boil, about 10 mins. Press Cancel.

4 Discard aromatics and water from the pot. In cold running water, rinse the pork bones clean and transfer to a large plate. Clean the inner pot with warm water.

5 In a large pot over high heat, bring 8 cups of water to a boil. Add whole cabbage and sea salt, cook for about 4 minutes, until the cabbage is soft and bright green. Rinse in cold running water or soak in an ice bath. Squeeze out excess liquid out by hand.

6 Add 6 cups of water to the inner pot and add the seasoning paste. Stir until dissolved. Add pork bones, potatoes, and cabbage.

7 Turn and lock the lid and move the steam release valve to the sealed position. Select Pressure Cook on High and program for 15 minutes. When the cooking is complete, release pressure naturally. Unlock and carefully remove the lid.

8 Add salt to taste. Garnish individual bowls with kkaennip, deulkkae garu, and scallion greens and serve.

galbitang 갈비탕

beef short rib soup

Serves 4

I think of this soup as a luxurious version of Sogogi Muguk (page 76). Since short ribs are a deluxe cut of meat, we tend to eat this on special occasions. It may be why this soup is often served at weddings. Before the 1970s and 80s, Janchi Guksu (page 48) was a common entrée served at weddings to symbolize longevity and happiness. As trends changed, galbitang became a popular dish served at weddings during the 90s. Lately, buffet lines at wedding receptions are trending. The Instant Pot tenderizes the meat and makes a clear but flavorful broth in much less time. - *Selina*

Prep Time / 20 min, plus 1 hr to soak

Pressure Cook Time / 20 min

Release / Natural

---

3 lbs beef short ribs, bone in, excess fat trimmed, and cut into 2-inch chunks

1 serving dangmyeon (sweet potato starch noodle)

5 garlic cloves

1 tbsp whole black peppercorns

2 bay leaves

½ small mu (Korean radish), peeled, quartered, and cut into ½-inch thick slices

2 scallions, stems cut into 1 ½-inch pieces, plus thin slices for garnish

4 dried jujubes (optional)

EGG JIDAN 지단 (optional)
2 large eggs
1 tsp cooking oil

---

1 Soak short ribs in cold water for 1 hour, draining and replacing the water every 20 minutes. Soak dangmyeon noodles in warm water for 20 minutes. Drain and set aside.

2 Using a strainer bag, add garlic, peppercorns, and bay leaves. In a large pot, add short ribs, strainer bag with aromatics, and 6 cups of water. Bring to boil, about 10 to 15 minutes. When the short ribs are par-boiled, use a spoon and skimmer to remove the strainer bag and discard the liquid. In cold running water, rinse and remove by hand any sediments remaining on the meat.

3 In the inner pot, add the short ribs, mu, scallion stems, jujubes (if using), and 8 cups of water

4 Turn and lock the lid and move the steam release valve to the sealed position. Select Pressure Cook on High and program for 20 minutes. When the cooking is complete, release pressure naturally. Unlock and carefully remove the lid

5 Select Saute on High and add dangmyeon. Cook it for 2 to 3 minutes.

6 Transfer the short ribs and dangmyeon into a separate bowl. Season the broth with salt and pepper to taste.

(recipe continues)

galbitang

갈비탕

beef short rib soup
(continued)

7 Ladle soup, short ribs, and dangmyeon into individual bowls. Garnish the soup with Egg Jidan (if using) and sliced scallions.

Tip For a more clear broth, refrigerate the broth overnight after Step 4. The solidified fat can be easily skimmed the next day.

To make Egg Jidan

1 In a small bowl, whisk eggs.

2 Using a small non-stick skillet, add cooking oil to thinly coat the surface. Over low heat, when the pan is hot, pour the egg mixture into the skillet. When the egg liquid begins to solidify, turn off the heat. Let the egg crepe sit in the hot pan, about 2 to 3 minutes. Turn the heat on to low heat. Flip over the egg crepe and let the other side finish cooking, about 1 to 2 minutes.

3 Allow the egg to cool, then cut into thin strips.

miyeok guk 미역국

seaweed soup

Serves 4 to 6

Miyeok guk is a very common household soup, yet a very symbolic one. This soup is traditionally consumed by Korean mothers after giving birth. It is nutrient-dense with calcium and iodine, and proven to be nourishing for nursing mothers. This soup is typically eaten on birthdays as a way to celebrate your mother giving birth to you. After giving birth to my child, I remember my mother made me drink this soup, like it was tea, for 3 weeks straight. It's a good thing that I have never and never will get sick of eating it. It's comforting on all levels. - *Selina*

Prep Time / 5 min
Pressure Cook Time / 10 min
Release / Quick

1 cup dried miyeok (seaweed), preferably precut small pieces

2 tsp sesame oil

½ lb beef ribeye steak, cut into ½-inch chunks

1 tbsp guk ganjang (soup soy sauce)

1 tsp fish sauce

1 tsp minced garlic

1 Soak miyeok in a large bowl of water at room temperature until it becomes soft, about 5 minutes. Wash miyeok in cold running water, drain out excess liquid.

2 Preheat the Instant Pot on the Sauté setting. When the inner pot is heated, add sesame oil and beef. Add miyeok and cook until the beef browns, about 5 minutes. Add guk ganjang, fish sauce, garlic, and cook, about 2 to 3 minutes. Add 6 cups of water.

3 Turn and lock the lid and move the steam release valve to the sealed position. Select Pressure Cook on High, program for 10 minutes. When the cooking is complete, quick-release pressure manually. Unlock and carefully remove the lid.

4 Season with salt to taste and serve.

Tips

- Once soaked, dried miyeok expands in large volumes. Precut miyeok is available for purchase but if large miyeok sheets are used, cut soaked miyeok into small pieces.

- Miyeok guk with beef can spoil quickly so freeze for storing up to a month.

- For a vegetarian option, substitute the beef with dried shiitake mushrooms. Soak the mushrooms in water to expand and cook together with miyeok.

sogogi muguk 소고기 무국

beef and radish soup

Serves 6

Growing up, this soup was on weekly rotation at our house. I can see why, since my mom worked every day and this soup has just a few key ingredients. It's easy to make and when served with rice and some kimchi, you've got a meal. My mom never seasoned the meat before cooking, but I added some in the meat and broth for an extra bump of flavor. - *Nancy*

Prep Time / 15 min
Pressure Cook Time / 10 min
Release / Natural and Quick

1 lb beef brisket or chuck roast

3 tbsp guk ganjang (soup soy sauce), divided

3 tsp minced garlic, divided

1 tsp sesame oil

Pinch of ground black pepper

1 ½ lbs mu (Korean radish), or daikon, peeled, quartered and cut into ½-inch thick slices

3 scallions, thinly sliced

1 Cut the beef into bite-sized pieces, about ¼-inch thick, and add to a medium bowl. Add 2 tbsp of guk ganjang, 2 tsp garlic, sesame oil, and pepper to the beef and mix well together. Set aside for 10 minutes.

2 Preheat the Instant Pot on the Sauté setting. When the inner pot is hot, add the marinated beef and sauté until the meat is browned on all sides, about 3 to 4 minutes. Add 10 cups of water and mu to the inner pot.

3 Turn and lock the lid and move the steam release valve to the sealed position. Select Pressure Cook on High, and program for 10 minutes. When the cooking is complete, release pressure naturally for 5 minutes and quick-release the remaining pressure. Unlock and carefully remove the lid.

4 With a spoon, remove any scum that froths to the top of the broth. Add remaining garlic, guk ganjang, and scallions. Cook for 2 to 3 minutes or until the scallions have wilted.

5 Season with salt to taste. Do not add more guk ganjang as that will change your broth to a darker brown color.

6 Serve sogogi muguk with a side of rice.

baechu guk 배추국

napa cabbage soup

Serves 4 to 6

I typically make baechu guk in winters when napa cabbage is in season. Also known as kimjang season (shared efforts for kimchi-making), napa cabbage is found in abundance, so there's always enough cabbage to go around for this soup. Adding beef to this dish really deepens the flavor. - *Selina*

Prep Time / 10 min
Pressure Cook Time / 7 min
Release / Quick

½ small napa cabbage

2 tbsp doenjang

2 tsp gochugaru

2 tsp minced garlic

2 tbsp guk ganjang (soup soy sauce)

½ lb beef ribeye, cut into
   bite-sized pieces

2 scallions, cut into big chunks

1 Core and remove napa cabbage stems and separate the leaves. Cut the cabbage into large 2-inch square size pieces. Wash and rinse the cabbage in cold water then drain.

2 In a small bowl, combine doenjang, gochugaru, garlic, and guk ganjang to make the seasoning paste.

3 In the inner pot, add 6 cups of water and mix in the seasoning paste until dissolved. Add beef, cabbage, and scallions.

4 Turn and lock the lid and move the steam release valve to the sealed position. Select Pressure Cook and the Soup setting on High, and program for 7 minutes. When the cooking is complete, quick-release pressure manually. Unlock and carefully remove the lid.

5 Season with salt to taste and serve.

Tips

- Use a thicker cut of meat over thinly sliced meat.

- Cabbage releases excess water, so test the amount of water used when scaling this recipe. Use more doenjang and guk ganjang to season.

doenjang jjigae 된장찌개

soybean paste stew

Serves 4 to 6

My husband loves the salty and gamchilmat flavors in doenjang. For me, doenjang jjigae is miso soup's rough, tough-love auntie that always tells it to you straight. She never shies away and looks at you, dead straight in the eyes and tells you exactly what's up. She is bold, just like this stew. Doenjang jjigae is a bit pungent, savory, and can be spicy if you add hot chili peppers. Like many Korean stews, this soup needs to be accompanied with rice for balance or else, risk getting that look of disapproval from your auntie. - *Nancy*

Prep Time / 15 min
Pressure Cook Time / 5 min
Release / Quick

2 tsp oil, olive or vegetable

5 tbsp doenjang

¼ lb maitake or oyster mushrooms

1 to 2 tsp gochugaru, depending on spice preference

1 zucchini, diced into 1-inch pieces

1 ½ cups Yukon potatoes, diced into 1-inch pieces

½ medium yellow onion, diced

2 tsp minced garlic

1 (12 oz) block firm tofu, cut into 1-inch cubes

1 jalapeño pepper, cut into ¼ inch slices (optional)

4 cups rice water (see Glossary, page 165)

1 Preheat Instant Pot to the Sauté function on Low and add oil. When the oil is shimmering, add doenjang, mushrooms, and gochugaru. Sauté until doenjang is evenly distributed and mushrooms are soft, about 1 to 2 minutes.

2 Add zucchini, potatoes, onion, garlic, tofu, jalapeño pepper, and 4 cups of rice water.

3 Turn and lock the lid and move the steam release valve to the sealed position. Select Pressure Cook on High and program for 5 minutes. When the cooking is complete, quick-release pressure manually. Unlock and carefully remove the lid.

4 Add salt to taste. Serve with a side of rice.

Tip For a rice water substitute, use Man Neung Myeolchi Yooksu (page 139) or a low-sodium chicken broth. In a pinch, use water with 1 teaspoon of fish sauce.

budae jjigae 부대찌개

korean army stew

Serves 2 to 3

Budae jjigae may seem like a hodge-podge of a stew, but for me, it is comfort food. My mom didn't make this stew for us very often but my siblings and I loved eating Spam. I've come to value budae jjigae more since learning about its origins. After the war in the 1950s, food was scarce, and Koreans found ways to cook with the canned meat supply from U.S. Army bases, which is how the name "Korean army stew" or "army base stew" came to be. It's amazing to know that something created in survival mode is still a beloved dish. This stew has an anchovy and kimchi broth base and the flavor combination with processed meats really enhances when everything cooks and reduces down. Adding ramen noodles and a slice of cheese became a trend as it gained popularity in later years. - *Selina*

Prep Time / 20 min
Pressure Cook Time / 3 min
Release / Quick

1 tbsp minced garlic

2 tbsp gochugaru

1 tbsp soy sauce

1 tbsp fish sauce

1 tbsp mirin

1 cup soybean sprouts

½ (12 oz) block tofu, cut into thin squares

1 cup aged or sour kimchi, chopped

2 scallions, cut into matchstick pieces, plus thin slices for garnish

½ cup canned baked beans

1 (12 oz) can Spam, or canned meat, ⅔ block cut into small cubes

1 beef frank, sliced

4 cups Man Neung Myeolchi Yooksu (page 139)

1 pack dried instant ramen noodles

½ cup tteokguk tteok (coin-shaped sliced rice cakes)

1 slice, Kraft Singles cheese

1 In a small bowl, combine garlic, gochugaru, soy sauce, fish sauce, and mirin, and mix well until paste-like in consistency.

2 Lay the soybean sprouts across the bottom of the inner pot. Next, add a layer of tofu, then kimchi and scallions. Add canned beans, meat, and frankfurter slices. Add man neung myeolchi yooksu and pour the sauce on top. Do not stir.

3 Turn and lock the lid and move the steam release valve to the sealed position. Select Pressure Cook on Low and program for 3 minutes. When the cooking is complete, quick-release pressure manually. Unlock and carefully remove the lid.

4 Select the Sauté function on Low. Add ramen noodles and tteokguk tteok (if using) and cook, about 2 to 3 minutes. Add a slice of cheese on top and cover with the lid. Press Cancel.

5 Add scallion slices to garnish and serve.

Tips

- For larger servings, make the stew in smaller batches as many of the ingredients will overcook in the Instant Pot.

- For an authentic budae jjigae experience, place the pot at the table setting. Ladle portions from the pot directly into individual bowls to serve. Best served shared!

gochujang jjigae 고추장찌개

chili pepper paste stew

Serves 4

Gochujang jjigae is a memorable dish for me. It's a stew that my dad used to make for us in Korea when we would go camping by the creek. The camping memory is faint but the flavors of this dish are still very vivid to me. From time to time, I still talk about it with my dad. He always used canned corned beef so when St. Patrick's Day comes around every year, the combination of corned beef, potato, and cabbage takes me on a trip down memory lane. - *Selina*

Prep Time / 15 min
Pressure Cook Time / 3 min
Release / Quick

2 tbsp gochujang

1 tsp minced garlic

1 tbsp guk ganjang (soup soy sauce)

1 tbsp mirin

1 dashi pack (anchovies, kelp, dried shrimp)

1 (12 oz) canned corned beef

4 mini gold potatoes, cut into 1-inch pieces

1 small zucchini, cut into 1-inch pieces

¼ small cabbage, cut into 1-inch pieces

½ yellow onion, cut into 1-inch pieces

1 (12 oz) block of tofu, ½ of block cubed (optional)

1 scallion, chopped (optional)

1 In a small bowl, whisk gochuchang, minced garlic, guk ganjang, and mirin until well-combined to make the seasoning sauce.

2 Select Sauté on High. Add dashi pack and 2 ½ cups water. Bring to a boil for about 5 minutes. Select Cancel and remove the dashi pack. Add the sauce seasoning and ¾ of the can of corned beef and stir until the sauce is dissolved. Add potatoes, zucchini, cabbage, and onion. Mix well to combine.

3 Turn and lock the lid and move the steam release valve to the sealed position. Select Pressure Cook on High and program for 3 minutes. When the cooking is complete, quick-release pressure manually. Unlock and carefully remove the lid.

4 If using tofu, select Sauté on High and add tofu and scallions. Cook for 2 to 3 minutes.

5 Serve with rice and banchan on the side.

Tips

- Using the glass lid at Step 2 will help speed up cook time.

- Try using corned beef from the butcher instead of canned corned beef in this recipe.

kongbiji jjigae 콩비지 찌개

ground soybean stew

Serves 4 to 5

The ground soybeans in this stew create a thick texture and have a nutty flavor. A perfect spoonful includes a piece of pork, kimchi, a heaping amount of ground soybean, and a little bit of rice. I used pork ribs here because the Instant Pot does such a good job with cooking the ribs. - *Nancy*

Prep Time / 15 min, plus soaking time

Pressure Cook Time / 15 min

Release / Quick

½ cup dry meju kong (soybeans)

1 tbsp vegetable oil

1 ½ lbs pork ribs, sliced between the bones

¼ tsp kosher salt

2 tsp minced garlic

1 cup onion, diced

1 ½ cups kimchi, cut into bite-sized pieces

¼ cup kimchi juice (if available)

3 cups Man Neung Myeolchi Yooksu (page 139), or kelp, chicken, vegetable stock

1 tbsp guk ganjang (soup soy sauce)

2 scallions, thinly sliced

Special equipment: Blender

1 Rinse the meju kong and discard any rotten beans. In a large bowl, add meju kong and 2 cups of cold water. Soak for at least 6 hours to overnight. Refrigerate to avoid fermenting.

2 Select Sauté on High, and add the vegetable oil to the inner pot. When the oil is shimmering, add the pork ribs and brown evenly on all sides. Season with kosher salt. Transfer browned pork ribs to a plate and set aside.

3 Add the garlic and onion to the inner pot and sauté until the onions have softened. Add the kimchi and kimchi juice, and sauté until kimchi becomes soft, about 2 to 3 minutes. Return the pork ribs to the inner pot. Add Man Neung Myeolchi Yooksu and guk ganjang, and stir.

4 Turn and lock the lid and move the steam release valve to the sealed position. Select Pressure Cook on High and program for 15 minutes.

5 Add the soaked meju kong to a blender with 1 cup of water. Purée until evenly blended and creamy. Set aside.

6 When the cooking is complete, quick-release pressure manually. Unlock and carefully remove the lid and stir. Select the Sauté function on Low. Add the meju kong purée to the stew. Do not stir. When the meju kong purée starts to bubble, gently fold the mixture. Carefully, keep stirring occasionally, about 5 to 8 minutes. Do not cover.

7 Once the meju kong purée has fully cooked and the stew starts to bubble, add salt to taste and press Cancel.

8 Stir the stew, transfer to serving bowls, and add scallions. Serve immediately with a side of rice.

4

meat

Galbijjim, page 86

galbijjim
갈비찜
braised short ribs
86

maeun galbijjim
매운 갈비찜
braised spicy short ribs
87

bossam & musaengchae
보쌈 & 무생채
pork belly cabbage wraps with spicy radish salad
89

gogi wanja
고기완자
korean meatballs
92

dwaeji bulgogi
돼지불고기
spicy pork
94

dwaeji deung galbi
돼지등갈비
pork baby back ribs
95

jjusam bulgogi
쭈삼불고기
spicy baby octopus & pork stir fry
97

maple syrup bulgogi
매이플시럽 불고기
98

sous-vide steak with soy chili sauce
수비드 스테이크
99

jokbal
족발
braised pig trotters
102

kimchi jjim
김치찜
braised pork & aged kimchi
103

dong pa yook
동파육
korean-chinese chashu pork
104

galbijjim 갈비찜

braised short ribs

Serves 4 to 6

I don't know anyone that doesn't like galbijjim. It's a special dish eaten on holidays like New Year's Day or Chuseok (Korean Thanksgiving). If I had to choose one dish that benefits most from using the Instant Pot, it's galbijjim. Typically, this recipe takes hours to make, but it takes me just 20 minutes of pressure cooking time with the Instant Pot! I think that alone is something to celebrate. - *Selina*

Prep Time / 15 min, plus 1 hr to soak
Pressure Cook Time / 20 min
Release / Quick

4 lbs beef short ribs, excess fat trimmed and cut into big chunks

½ yellow onion, peeled

4 garlic cloves

1 (1-inch) piece of ginger, peeled and sliced

3 Yukon Gold potatoes, cut in half

1 medium carrot, peeled and cut into 1-inch pieces

⅓ small mu, peeled and cut into 1 ½-inch pieces

4 pearl onions, peeled

SAUCE

½ cup soy sauce

½ cup water

2 tbsp mirin

1 tbsp plum extract syrup

2 tbsp white granulated sugar

½ Asian pear or apple, grated or juiced (optional)

1 Place the short ribs in a large bowl. Cover with cold water and soak for about 1 hour, draining and replacing the water every 20 minutes.

2 In the inner pot, add short ribs, onion, garlic, ginger, and 6 cups of water.

3 Turn and lock the lid and move the steam release valve to the sealed position. Select Pressure Cook on High and program for 10 minutes. When the cooking is complete, quick-release pressure manually. Unlock and carefully remove the lid.

4 Using tongs, transfer the short ribs to a dish and discard any remaining solids and liquids in the pot. Rinse the pot with warm water.

5 In a small bowl, whisk the sauce ingredients until well-combined. In the inner pot, add potatoes, carrots, mu, pearl onions, sauce mixture, and ½ cup of water.

6 Turn and lock the lid in place with the steam release valve into a sealed position. Select Pressure Cook on Low and program for 10 minutes. When the cooking is complete, quick-release pressure manually. Unlock and carefully remove the lid.

7 Plate the meat and vegetables in a serving bowl. Pour the remaining cooked sauce over the galbijjim to keep it moist.

Tip When preparing the root vegetables, shave off hard edges with a vegetable peeler to prevent vegetables from turning into mush.

maeun galbijjim 매운 갈비찜

spicy braised short ribs

Serves 4

This recipe is inspired by a famous dish from Sun Nong Dan in Los Angeles: spicy galbijjim with melted cheese on top. Going to Koreatown in L.A. is one of my favorite things to do in Southern California. For me, it's the closest thing to Korea without traveling overseas. Whenever I visit, I check out the food scene for new and hot trends. It's a wonderful change from traditional cuisine if you are looking for something familiar, but with a twist. And yes, it's definitely Instagram-worthy. Let's see your best cheese pull! - *Selina*

Prep Time / 15 min, plus 1 hr
   to soak
Pressure Cook Time / 13 min
Release / Quick

4 lbs beef short ribs, excess fat trimmed and cut into big chunks

1 small onion, peeled, cut in half

6 garlic cloves

1 (1-inch) piece of ginger, sliced

1 tbsp cooking oil

8 to 10 tteokbokki tteok (rice cakes), 2-inch cylinder pieces

2 yellow potatoes, thick ½-inch slices

6 dried red chilis

½ cup shredded mozzarella cheese

SAUCE

1 tbsp gochujang

1 tbsp gochugaru powder

¼ cup soy sauce

¼ tsp ground black pepper

1 tbsp minced garlic

2 tbsp mirin

1 tbsp oligodang (sweet syrup)

1 tbsp white granulated sugar

Special equipment: kitchen torch (optional)

1 Place the short ribs in a large bowl. Cover with cold water and soak for about 1 hour, draining and replacing the water every 20 minutes.

2 In the inner pot, add short ribs, onion, garlic, ginger, and 6 cups of water.

3 Turn and lock the lid and move the steam release valve to the sealed position. Select Pressure Cook on High and program for 10 min. When the cooking is complete, quick-release pressure manually. Unlock and carefully remove the lid.

4 Using tongs, transfer the short ribs to a dish and discard any remaining solids and liquids in the pot. Rinse the pot with warm water.

5 In a small frying pan, add cooking oil over medium-high heat. Add tteok and fry until crispy golden brown, about 5 to 7 minutes.

6 In a small bowl, whisk all sauce ingredients to combine. Add potatoes, dried chilis, 1 cup of sauce, and ½ cup of water to the inner pot.

(recipe continues)

maeun galbijjim

매운 갈비찜

braised spicy short ribs
(continued)

7 Turn and lock the lid and move the steam release valve to the sealed position. Select Pressure Cook on Low and program for 3 minutes. When the cooking is complete, quick-release pressure manually. Unlock and carefully remove the lid.

8 Add pan-fried tteok to the pot and gently mix to combine.

9 Transfer the meat and vegetables to a baking dish, top with meat juices and sprinkled cheese. With a torch (if using), slowly melt the cheese until it becomes stretchy.

Tips

- For frozen tteok, soak in a heat-safe bowl of hot water for about 10 minutes, and drain before using.

- For a torching substitute, place in a preheated oven at 400°F for 5 minutes until the cheese has melted.

bossam & musaengchae

보쌈 & 무생채

pork belly cabbage wraps and spicy radish salad

Serves 6

Bossam is truly a family-style dish, everyone makes their own custom pork belly bundles. Each layer is assembled according to preference: tuck meat into a leaf of lettuce or salted cabbage and endless fixings to top the bundles. I like to stuff mine with raw garlic slices, chili slices, sauces, and oysters, and try my hardest to fit it into one bite. Sometimes I win, but sometimes the bundles win and end up all over my hands and face! - *Nancy*

Prep Time / 1 hr
Pressure Cook Time / 25 min
Release / Quick

CABBAGE LEAVES

1 cup fine sea salt

1 small napa cabbage, cored and
   quartered

PORK BELLY

1 medium onion, quartered

3 large scallion stems (save green
   parts for salad)

1 (1-inch) piece ginger, peeled and cut
   in half

8 cloves garlic

2 bay leaves

2 tbsp doenjang

1 tsp whole black peppercorns

1 tsp kosher salt

½ cup brewed coffee

½ cup stout or porter beer

3 lbs pork belly, cut into 3-inch
   wide strips

(continued)

To prepare the cabbage

1 In a large bowl, mix 8 cups of water and sea salt until the salt has dissolved. Add the cabbage and soak for 1 to 2 hours. If the cabbage leaves are not fully submerged, make sure the leafy white parts are fully covered in the bath.

2 When the cabbage leaves are limp, lightly rinse and drain well. Set aside until ready to serve.

To cook the pork belly

1 Add onion, scallions, ginger, garlic, bay leaves, doenjang, black peppercorns, kosher salt, coffee, stout, and 3 cups of water to the inner pot. Select Sauté on High and simmer the stock for 3 minutes. Press Cancel. Add the pork belly to the inner pot in one layer.

2 Turn and lock the lid and move the steam release valve to the sealed position. Select Pressure Cook on High and program for 25 minutes. When the cooking is complete, quick-release pressure manually. Unlock and carefully remove the lid.

3 Remove the pork belly and discard the liquid and aromatics. Set the pork on a cutting board. When cool enough to handle, cut the pork into ¼-inch slices.

(recipe continues)

MUSAENGCHAE 무생채

1 lb mu (Korean radish), peeled and
  cut into matchsticks

3 tbsp gochugaru

1 tbsp roasted sesame seeds

1 tbsp minced garlic

½ tsp kosher salt

1 tsp sugar

2 tsp fish sauce

2 scallions, thinly sliced

Fresh oysters (optional)

ACCOMPANIMENTS

Saeujeot Jang (page 156)

Ssamjang (page 155)

Kkaennip (perilla), or shiso leaves

Garlic cloves, sliced thinly

Fresh chiles, sliced thinly

To make the musaengchae

1 In a large bowl, place mu in a large bowl and sprinkle with kosher salt. Toss to coat evenly. Set aside for 5 minutes.

2 In a small bowl, add gochugaru, roasted sesame seeds, garlic, kosher salt, sugar, and fish sauce, and mix until well-combined.

3 Drain mu and gently squeeze out any excess water by hand and return to the large bowl.

4 Add the seasoning paste to mu and mix to combine. Add scallions and toss. Gently mix in fresh oysters (if using) into the salad.

To serve

Plate the sliced pork belly on a large platter. Neatly arrange the cabbage leaves with a generous pile of musaengchae next to the pork. In separate small bowls, serve with saeujeot jang, ssamjang, and accompaniments (if using).

Tip

- As an alternative to the salted cabbage wraps, use leafy greens, like red leaf lettuce.

- Saeujeot is very salty. Use only tiny amounts on each pork wrap.

gogi wanja 고기완자

korean meatballs

Makes about 24 meatballs

This is a crowd favorite. I usually make this without gochujang for my kid and his friends or large gatherings, but you can totally include it. We often eat the meatballs with a side of rice and banchan as a meal. But dudes, these are also very tasty in a roll with some slaw and hot sauce. So. Tasty. - *Nancy*

Prep Time / 40 min

Pressure Cook Time / 5 min

Release / Quick

1 lb ground beef

½ lb ground pork

1 egg

½ cup panko breadcrumbs

½ cup minced onion

½ cup minced fresh shiitake mushrooms, stems removed

2 scallions, thinly sliced

4 garlic cloves, minced

1 tbsp soy sauce

1 tsp sesame oil

1 tsp kosher salt

½ tsp ground black pepper

1 tbsp vegetable oil

2 tbsp cornstarch

1 tsp roasted sesame seeds (optional)

1 tbsp pine nuts (optional)

SAUCE

¼ cup brown sugar

⅓ cup soy sauce

¼ cup mirin

¼ cup rice wine, or sake

3 tbsp (sweet syrup)

1 tsp minced ginger

1 tsp sesame oil

2 tsp gochujang (optional)

1 In a large bowl, combine beef, pork, egg, breadcrumbs, onion, mushrooms, scallions, garlic, soy sauce, sesame oil, kosher salt, and black pepper together. Shape the meat into 1½-inch balls.

2 Heat a pan to medium-high heat and add vegetable oil. When the oil is shimmering, add half of the meatballs to the pan and brown on all sides, about 3 to 5 minutes per batch. Do not cook fully through. Transfer to a plate and set aside. Repeat with the second batch of meatballs.

3 Add the sauce ingredients and ½ cup of water into the inner pot. Select the Sauté function on High. Simmer the sauce for about 2 to 3 minutes and stir well. Press Cancel. Add the meatballs and gently combine to evenly coat.

4 Turn and lock the lid and move the steam release valve to the sealed position. Select Pressure Cook on High and program for 5 minutes.

5 In a small bowl, mix 2 tablespoons of water with cornstarch until it dissolves.

6 When the cooking is complete, quick-release pressure manually. Unlock and carefully remove the lid.

7 Select Sauté on High. Add the cornstarch slurry to the meatballs. Gently stir until the sauce thickens, about 1 to 2 minutes.

8 Transfer the meatballs to a serving dish. Garnish with roasted sesame seeds, scallions, and pine nuts (if using) and serve.

dwaeji bulgogi 돼지불고기

spicy pork

Serves 4 to 5

My mother wasn't a fan of pork so she didn't make dwaeji bulgogi often, but thank goodness my aunt who lived nearby loved making this dish. This Instant Pot version cuts the marinating time and produces more sauce than the stove-top version. The spicy marinade pairs perfectly with the fatty pork. For maximum flavor and experience, eat it with lettuce wraps, toppings, and rice. Don't forget to spoon the delicious sauce over rice, too! This dish paired with light and refreshing banchan like Samsaek Namul (page 23), Geotjeori Kimchi (page 20) or Oi Kimchi (page 28), also makes a great spread. - *Nancy*

Prep Time / 15 min
Pressure Cook Time / 1 min
Release / Quick

MARINADE

½ large Asian pear, peeled and diced

¼ medium onion, diced

3 tbsp gochujang

2 tsp gochugaru

1 tbsp sugar

1 tbsp oligodang (sweet syrup)

2 tbsp mirin

3 garlic cloves

1 tbsp soy sauce

1 tbsp sesame oil

½ tsp minced ginger

1 tsp kosher salt

Pinch of ground black pepper

2 lbs pork belly, thinly sliced, about ⅛-inch thick

2 scallions, coarsely chopped

1 tsp roasted sesame seeds (optional)

Special equipment: Blender

1 In a blender, add 1 tablespoon of water and marinade ingredients. Blend until smooth.

2 Pour the marinade and add the pork into the inner pot. Combine together to evenly coat.

3 Turn and lock the lid and move the steam release valve to the sealed position. Select Pressure Cook on Low and program for 1 minute. When the cooking is complete, quick-release pressure manually. Unlock and carefully remove the lid.

4 Select the Sauté function on High. Add the scallions and sauté with the pork, about 1 minute.

5 Transfer to a serving dish and garnish with roasted sesame seeds (if using). Serve with rice.

Tip

- Serve this dish with rice, Ssamjang (page 155), and lettuce to make lettuce wraps.

- Add toppings like thin raw garlic slices, sliced chili peppers, or kkaennip (perilla) leaves.

dwaeji deung galbi 돼지등갈비

pork baby back ribs

Serves 4

Dwaeji deung galbi is a hit in our house. My young son doesn't have a tolerance for spicy foods, so these ribs are savory and full of flavor, but still mild enough for everyone at the table to enjoy. Begin with preparing the glaze and make the ribs while the glaze is simmering. For best results, finish the ribs in the oven for a sticky, caramelized, candied glaze. You don't have to wait for the meat to marinate so you'll save time. Plus, the ribs are cooked to perfection in the Instant Pot. I admit, we like to stuff our bellies full with these ribs. We rarely have leftovers. - *Nancy*

Prep Time / 15 min
Pressure Cook Time / 16 min
Release / Natural and Quick

GLAZE

½ cup soy sauce

¼ cup packed brown sugar

¼ cup mirin

¼ cup rice wine, or sake

¼ cup maple syrup

1 tsp grated ginger

1 tsp minced garlic

2 tbsp sesame oil

RIBS

1 (2 to 2½ lbs) rack baby back ribs

2 tsp kosher salt

¼ tsp ground black pepper

½ tsp garlic powder

¼ cup apple cider vinegar

Special equipment: baking sheet

To make the glaze

1 In a small saucepan, whisk glaze ingredients and 2 tablespoons of water until well-combined.

2 Simmer on low heat, stirring occasionally, for about 30 to 35 minutes and take the pan off heat. Set it aside. It will thicken as it cools.

3 Once cooled, whisk in the sesame oil until well-combined. Set aside.

To make the ribs

1 Prepare the ribs by removing the membrane from the underside of the ribs. Insert a paring knife underneath the membrane to help lift enough to grip. Slide it off by hand to remove. If it is very slippery, use a paper towel to help grip the membrane before removing. Or, ask the butcher to remove the membrane at the time of purchase.

2 In a small bowl, mix the kosher salt, black pepper, and garlic powder together.

3 Season both sides of the ribs with the dry seasoning.

4 Place the steamer rack inside the inner pot. Add apple cider vinegar and 1 cup of water.

(recipe continues)

dwaeji deung galbi

돼지등갈비

pork baby back ribs

(continued)

5 Place the ribs on top of the steamer rack, rolling them into a coil to fit.

6 Turn and lock the lid and move the steam release valve to the sealed position. Select Pressure Cook on High and program for 16 minutes (18 to 20 minutes for a more tender meat that falls off the bone). When the cooking is complete, release pressure naturally for 5 minutes and quick-release the remaining pressure. Unlock and carefully remove the lid.

7 Preheat the oven to 450°F degrees.

8 Line a baking sheet with foil and transfer the ribs to the baking sheet. Generously brush glaze on both sides of the ribs. Set aside some leftover glaze. Place the ribs in the oven and cook for about 2 minutes on each side, or until the sauce has caramelized and browned.

9 Remove ribs from the oven and brush the remaining glaze on the ribs. Serve with a side of rice.

jjusam bulgogi 쭈삼불고기

spicy baby octopus & pork stir fry

Serves 4

It's quite amusing to me that Koreans like to use shortened names or abbreviated words. When it comes to food, it often happens when the dish combines two unique ingredients that are not traditionally paired together: Jju is from jjukkumi (baby octopus), and sam from samgyeopsal (pork belly). Marinated in a gochujang-based sauce, the tender and juicy baby octopus and pork wrapped in kkaennip leaves with rice is a perfect bite. - *Selina*

Prep Time / 10 min
Pressure Cook Time / 8 min
Release / Quick

¾ lb baby octopus, thawed and cleaned (preferrably purchased with heads and tentacles separated)

1 lb pork belly, thinly sliced, and cut into 3-inch pieces

2 tbsp cooking oil

1 tbsp sesame oil

2 tsp roasted sesame seeds

2 bundles kkaennip (perilla) leaves (optional)

MARINADE

3 tbsp gochujang

2 tbsp gochugaru

3 tbsp sweet rice syrup

3 tbsp mirin

1 tbsp soy sauce

1 tbsp fish sauce

1 tsp ginger juice

1 tbsp minced garlic

½ tsp ground black pepper

1 Using a colander, rinse baby octopus and drain any excess liquid.

2 In a large mixing bowl, whisk the marinade ingredients until well-combined into a smooth and thin consistency. Add the pork and baby octopus, and evenly coat with sauce.

3 Place the marinated pork and baby octopus into the inner pot.

4 Turn and lock the lid and move the steam release valve to the sealed position. Select Pressure Cook on High and program for 8 minutes. When the cooking is complete, quick-release pressure manually. Unlock and carefully remove the lid.

5 Using a slotted spoon, transfer the cooked pork and baby octopus to a dish and set aside. Discard remaining liquid and rinse the pot with hot water. Place the pork and baby octopus in the pot.

6 Select the Sauté function on High and add cooking oil. Cook until the mixture starts to caramelize, about 5 minutes.

7 Place the pork and baby octopus in a dish. Drizzle sesame oil and sprinkle sesame seeds on top. Serve with kkaennip (if using) and freshly cooked rice for wraps.

Tip If thinly cut pork belly strips are not readily accessible, ask the local butcher to slice at a shabu cut (3.0 mm).

maple syrup bulgogi

매이플시럽 불고기

Serves 4 to 6

Here is my take on bulgogi using maple syrup and ground beef. I frequently use this as the main protein for bibimbap. I find it easy to mix together with other veggies and the flavor isn't as over-powering. You can combine to assemble a complete bibimbap dish (page 24) with freshly made rice, Samsaek Namul (page 23), and Bibimjang (page 154). - *Selina*

Prep Time / 20 min
Pressure Cook Time / 2 min
Release / Quick

MARINADE

½ cup soy sauce

¼ cup maple syrup

1 tsp sesame oil

2 tsp garlic, minced

1 tsp ginger juice

1 lb ground beef (80% lean, 20% fat)

¼ cup pine nuts

1 tbsp sesame oil

Special equipment: mortar and pestle

1 In a medium bowl, whisk the marinade ingredients until well-combined. Add the ground beef and combine. Marinate in the refrigerator for 30 minutes.

2 On a small skillet over medium-low heat, toast pine nuts until lightly brown, about 10 minutes. Using a mortar and pestle, coarsely grind the pine nuts. Set aside.

3 In the inner pot, add the marinated ground beef.

4 Turn and lock the lid and move the release valve to the sealed position. Select Pressure Cook on High and program for 2 minutes. When the cooking is complete, quick-release pressure manually. Unlock and carefully remove the lid.

5 Add sesame oil and select Sauté on High, and continue to cook the beef until it caramelizes, about 2 to 3 minutes.

6 Transfer the beef to a serving dish and top with ground pine nuts. Serve with rice or noodles.

Tip Substitute ground beef for a thin sliced ribeye for a more traditional-style dish. The ground beef is more versatile and works well with rice, noodles, and soups.

sous-vide steak with soy chili sauce 수비드 스테이크

Serves 4

I know, I know, I know... this is not a traditional Korean dish. But if you're new to sous-vide and have the sous-vide function on your Instant Pot, you might as well try it! Get your desired doneness: juicy, tender, and evenly cooked with precision—to perfection. Let the Instant Pot do all the work and all that's left is a quick sear for some nice browning on the outside. The side sauce is garlicky, sweet, and salty, with a little kick from the chili peppers. - *Nancy*

Prep Time / 15 min

Sous-Vide Cook Time / 1 to 3 hrs (depending on desired cook time)

2 ribeye or New York strip steaks, 1½ to 2-inches thick

1 tsp vegetable oil

SOY CHILI SAUCE

3 tsp sesame oil

2 tsp minced garlic

1 tsp minced ginger

¼ cup soy sauce

3 tbsp mirin

3 tbsp rice wine, or sake

3 tbsp brown sugar

2 tbsp oligodang (sweet syrup)

¼ tsp ground black pepper

1 green serrano or jalapeño pepper, diced

1 red jalapeño pepper, diced

1 scallion, thinly sliced

1 tsp roasted sesame seeds

3 tbsp fresh lemon juice

Special equipment: cast iron skillet, vacuum sealer and bags, or gallon size resealable bags (like Ziplock)

1 Fill the inner pot with warm water, between the 3- to 4-quart lines.

2 Put the lid on with the valve at the vent position. Select the Sous-Vide function and program the temperature and cooking time to preferred doneness (see Cooking Tables, page 166). (I like to cook 1½-inch steaks at 131° F for 1½ hours). Press Start.

3 Generously season the steaks, including the sides and edges, with salt and pepper. Add the steaks to individual seal bags and seal the bags using a vacuum sealer. (If you do not have a vacuum sealer, use resealable bags with the water displacement method on page 100).

4 When the water comes to temperature, submerge the steaks, side by side, inside the water while making sure the pouches have enough room in between and on the sides. (If you are using resealable bags, make sure the zipper is at the top and above the water line.) Turn the lid back on with the valve on the vent position.

(recipe continues)

sous-vide steak with soy chili sauce
수비드 스테이크
(continued)

5 In a small saucepan on medium heat, add sesame oil, garlic, and ginger and cook, about 1 minute without browning or burning. Add soy sauce, mirin, rice wine, brown sugar, oligodang, black pepper, and ⅓ cup water to the saucepan. Stir occasionally until the sugar dissolves, then simmer on medium-low to medium heat, about 5 minutes. Stir in the chili peppers, scallions, sesame seeds, and lemon juice. Turn off heat and pour into a bowl and set aside.

6 When the sous-vide cooking time is complete, take the steaks out and remove them from the bags. Pat the steaks dry with paper towels.

7 When sous-vide steaks are cooked to temperature, it may be dull in color and need browning. Add vegetable oil to a cast iron pan or skillet on high heat. When the pan is hot, add the steaks and sear one side for about 15 to 30 seconds. Avoid searing the steaks for too long to prevent overcooking. Sear the other side for another 15 to 30 seconds. Repeat for steak edges.

8 Transfer the steak to a cutting board and cut into strips for serving.

9 Place the steak strips on a plate and drizzle soy chili sauce on top. Serve with rice and banchan.

water displacement method

If using resealable bags, place one steak per gallon size bag. Seal the bag, leaving a small opening. Fill a large pot or bowl with water and slowly lower the pouch into the water. The water pressure will push the air out of the bag. As the bag is lowered into the water, remove as much air as possible. Submerge until the zipper is right above the water line. Once the air is removed, finish sealing the bag.

jokbal 족발

braised pig trotters

Serves 4 to 6

A survey in a Korean publication rated late-night delivery foods. The most popular snack was jokbal, followed by dakbal (spicy chicken feet). You might be wondering: what's with all the feet? If you're familiar with soju drinking culture, you might understand. I'm not going to lie, this recipe may be a challenge. It uses less common ingredients in Korean cooking, like star anise and cloves, and the process of pyeon yook (shaping meat into a mold) may be unfamiliar. But when you have your first bite with a shot of soju, you'll know it was all worth it. Jjan! ('Cheers!') - *Selina*

Prep Time / 5 min, plus 1 hour to soak

Pressure Cook Time / 20 min, plus 20 min to boil

Release / Quick

---

2 to 3 lbs pig trotters

2 tbsp doenjang

1 onion, halved

1 (2-inch) ginger, peeled and sliced

6 garlic cloves

1 tbsp black peppercorns, in strainer bag

2 bay leaves

¼ cup soy sauce

2 tbsp dark soy sauce

2 tbsp mirin

¼ cup oligodang (sweet syrup)

1 whole apple, halved

4 star anise

2 cinnamon sticks

1 tbsp whole cloves

Special equipment: plastic wrap

---

1 Rinse and soak the pig trotters in cold water for at least 1 hour. Discard and replace the water once.

2 Select Sauté on High and add 6 cups of water to the inner pot. Add doenjang, and mix to dissolve. Add pig trotters, onion, ginger, garlic, peppercorns, and bay leaves. Bring it to boil for about 20 minutes. Press Cancel. With tongs, transfer the pig trotters into a bowl. Discard the liquid and aromatics. Rinse the pig trotters in cold running water to remove any impurities. Rinse the pot with warm water.

3 In the inner pot, add pig trotters, soy sauce, dark soy sauce, mirin, oligodang, apple, star anise, cinnamon sticks, cloves, and 2 cups of water.

4 Turn and lock the lid and move the steam release valve to the sealed position. Select Meat (Pork) on High and program for 20 minutes. When the cooking is complete, quick-release pressure manually. Transfer the meat onto a tray to cool. Once cool enough to touch, pull the meat off the bone by hand, it should come off easily.

5 Lay plastic wrap over a cutting board. Place the trotter meat, skin side down. Tightly wrap the trotter to mold into a log. Wrap it several times for an airtight mold. Refrigerate for 1 to 2 hours before cutting it into thin slices to serve.

6 Serve with Saeujeot Sauce (page 156), sliced garlic, lettuce wrap, and soju.

kimchi jjim 김치찜

braised pork & aged kimchi

Serves 4

Mugeunji (aged kimchi) is usually fermented for 6 months or longer. The salt brine turns the cabbage sour and soft, and nearly translucent. It's typically too pungent to eat on its own so it's commonly served in braised or stewed dishes. Kimchi jjim flavors are deeper and more intense than good ol' classic Kimchi Jjigae (page 62). Keeping the cabbage core intact not only adds a rustic touch but also allows the leaves to tenderize and soak up the fats and flavors from the pork belly without turning to mush. The tenderness from the pork paired with the sour kimchi makes the perfect complement of acid, salt, and fat. Rice water and saeujeot are all you need to make this dish really tasty. It's a must-try! - *Selina*

Prep Time / 30 min
Pressure Cook Time / 10 min
Release / Natural and Quick

1 lb pork belly, uncut

½ lb pork shoulder, uncut

2 tbsp mirin

1 tbsp ginger juice

½ tsp ground black pepper

1 (18 oz) pouch mugeunji (aged kimchi, preferrably Jongga brand)

3 cups rice water (see Glossary, page 165)

SAUCE

3 tbsp gochugaru

1 tbsp mirin

1 tbsp guk ganjang (soup soy sauce)

2 tsp minced garlic

2 tsp minced saeujeot (salted shrimp) or fish sauce

1 tsp ginger juice

1 tsp sugar

½ tsp ground black pepper

1 In a medium bowl, add the pork belly, pork shoulder, mirin, ginger juice, and black pepper. Mix to combine. Place in the refrigerator, about 30 minutes.

2 In a small bowl, whisk all ingredients for the sauce and stir until well-combined.

3 Quickly rinse mugeunji in running water or dunk in a bowl of cold water for a few seconds to remove excess seasoning and juice.

4 In the inner pot, add mugeunji, pork belly and pork shoulder, sauce, and rice water.

5 Turn and lock the lid and move the steam release valve to the sealed position. Select Pressure Cook on High and program for 10 minutes. When the cooking is complete, release pressure naturally for 5 minutes, then quick-release any remaining pressure.

6 Transfer the pork belly and pork shoulder to a cutting board. Slice into ¼-inch thick pieces. Using tongs and scissors, remove the core from mugeunji and cut into strips.

7 Place the pork and mugeunji in a deep serving platter and top with juices. Serve with rice.

dong pa yook 동파육

korean-chinese chasu pork

Serves 4

Dong pa yook, also known as dong po rou in Chinese, may not be a classic Korean-Chinese dish but it's still a popular dish. Korean-Chinese cuisine developed and flourished after Chinese immigrants settled in Korea and a new kind of cuisine emerged to satisfy the Korean palate. Jjajangmyeon (page 45) and Jjamppong (page 132) are the most iconic dishes. I love the way the Instant Pot tenderizes the pork belly for this dish. The savory and sweet flavors from the dark soy and oyster sauces add loads of gamchilmat. - *Selina*

Prep Time / 5 min
Pressure Cook Time / 10 min
Release / Natural and Quick

3 bok choy, cut in half or quarters

Pinch of fine sea salt

1½ lbs pork belly

6 garlic cloves

1 (1 ½ -inch) piece of ginger, peeled and sliced

2 bay leaves

1 tsp whole black peppercorns

2 tbsp dark soy sauce

1 tbsp soy sauce

1 tbsp oyster sauce

1 tbsp mirin

1 tbsp brown sugar

2 tsp ginger juice

1 Using a medium pot over high heat, bring 4 cups of water to a boil. Add a pinch of salt. Blanch the bok choy until the leaves turn soft and bright green, about 3 to 4 minutes.

2 In a medium bowl, prepare an ice bath with cold water and ice. Shock the bok choy in the ice water. Squeeze out the excess liquid and set aside.

3 In the inner pot, add pork, garlic, ginger, bay leaves, peppercorns, and 8 cups of water.

4 Turn and lock the lid and move the steam release valve to the sealed position. Select Pressure Cook on High and program for 10 minutes. When the cooking is complete, release pressure naturally for 10 minutes, then quick-release any remaining pressure. Unlock and carefully remove the lid. Discard the liquid and aromatics, then rinse the inner pot with warm water.

5 In the inner pot, add dark soy sauce, soy sauce, oyster sauce, mirin, brown sugar, ginger juice, and 1 cup of water. Stir to combine well. Select Sauté on Low. Add the pork belly and simmer until the sauce reduces by nearly half, about 5 to 10 minutes. Flip the meat over several times.

6 Remove the pork belly and cut into thin slices. Serve with bok choy and rice.

Tip During preparation, if any hairs remain on the pork skin, shave off with disposable razors.

5

chicken

Jjimdak, page 108

jjimdak
찜닭
braised chicken
108

dakbokkeumtang
닭볶음탕
spicy chicken stew
109

samgyetang
삼계탕
ginseng chicken soup
111

dak kalguksu
닭칼국수
chicken with noodles soup
112

dak gaejang
닭개장
spicy chicken soup
114

dak hanmari
닭한마리
chicken hot pot with noodles
115

chogae guksu
초계국수
cold chicken breast noodles
116

dak galbi
닭갈비
spicy chicken stir-fry
118

dak jook
닭죽
chicken porridge
119

chicken curry
치킨카레
121

jjimdak 찜닭

braised chicken

Serves 4

My stomach is growling, and my mouth is watering just thinking about this dish. You can think of jjimdak as the chicken version of Galbijjim (page 86). It has a similar flavor profile with a little bit of a kick from the red chili peppers. It's known to have originated from the southern part of Korea, in Andong, and became a popular chicken dish in the 80s. - *Selina*

Prep Time / 15 min
Pressure Cook Time / 10 min
Release / Quick

- 1 lb chicken drummettes, excess fat and skin trimmed
- 1 lb chicken thigh meat, excess fat and skin trimmed, cut into 2-inch chunks
- ½ tsp fine sea salt
- 2 tbsp soju or cooking sake
- ½ cup soy sauce
- 1 tbsp sweet rice syrup
- 2 tsp caramel syrup
- 1 tbsp white granulated sugar
- 3 Yukon Gold potatoes, cut into 1-inch pieces
- 1 medium carrot, cut into 1-inch pieces
- 4 cloves garlic, minced
- 2 scallions, chopped
- ¼ tsp black pepper
- 6 dried red chili peppers
- 1 serving dangmyeon (sweet potato starch noodles)

1 In a large bowl, season the chicken with the sea salt and soju and let sit for about 20 minutes. In a small bowl, combine soy sauce, sweet rice syrup, caramel syrup, and sugar. Mix well until the sugar and syrup have dissolved.

2 In the inner pot, add the chicken and 5 cups of water. Select Sauté on High and bring to a boil, for about 5 minutes. Press Cancel. Using a skimmer, remove the chicken. Under cold running water, rub off any impurities on the par-cooked chicken by hand. Pour the broth through a strainer into a separate bowl. Rinse the inner pot with warm water.

3 Add chicken, potatoes, carrots, and garlic into the inner pot. Add the sauce mixture and 1 cup of chicken broth.

4 Turn and lock the lid and move the steam release valve to the sealed position. Select Pressure Cook on High and program for 10 minutes.

5 In a small bowl, soak the chili peppers in water. In a medium bowl, soak the dangmyeon in warm water. Set aside for 10 minutes.

6 When the cooking is complete, quick-release pressure manually. Unlock and carefully remove the lid. Select the Sauté function on Low, add dangmyeon, red chili peppers, scallions, and black pepper. Cook for another 2 to 3 minutes, stirring occasionally.

7 Serve with rice.

Tip For a caramel syrup substitute, use a combination of dark soy sauce and brown sugar.

dakbokkeumtang 닭볶음탕

spicy chicken stew

Serves 4

From my childhood memories, dakbokkeumtang stands out the most. My mom still makes this dish for me because she knows how much I love it—from the salty sweet to the spiciness to the carrots. Yup, the carrots! They're soft, a little sweet, and soak up all the sauce. My mom often uses chicken drumsticks, but I prefer chicken thighs for the Instant Pot because it's easier to handle in the narrow pot. She never adds rice cakes, but when I look at the delicious sauce in the pot, it calls me to add some in. - *Nancy*

Prep Time / 25 min
Pressure Cook Time / 10 min
Release / Quick

16 tteokbokki tteok (rice cakes), 2-inch cylinder pieces (optional)
¼ cup gochugaru
¼ cup soy sauce
2 tbsp white granulated sugar
2 tbsp minced garlic
2 tbsp gochujang
2 tbsp rice wine, or sake
1 tsp kosher salt
¼ tsp ground black pepper
2 ½ lbs bone-in chicken thighs, cut into large chunks, fat trimmed
1 large onion, peeled and quartered
½ lb Yukon Gold potatoes, quartered
2 medium carrots, cut into 1 ½- to 2-inch pieces
1 tsp sesame oil
2 scallions, thinly sliced
Soy sauce, to taste

1 If using packaged tteokbokki tteok, soak in a bowl of cold water and set aside, about 10 minutes.

2 In the inner pot, add gochugaru, soy sauce, sugar, garlic, gochujang, rice wine, kosher salt, and black pepper. Mix well. Add the chicken to the sauce mixture and coat evenly. Add the onions, potatoes, and carrots and combine well. Add ¾ cup of water.

3 Turn and lock the lid and move the steam release valve to the sealed position. Select the Poultry setting and adjust the pressure to High, program for 10 minutes. When the cooking is complete, quick-release pressure manually. Unlock and carefully open the lid.

4 Drizzle in sesame oil, add the scallions, and gently mix together. Using a slotted spoon, transfer the chicken and vegetables to a serving bowl.

5 Select Sauté on High. Drain tteok (if using) and add to the sauce. Cook tteok until they are soft, about 2 to 3 minutes. If tteok are omitted, let the sauce reduce, about 3 minutes. Taste the sauce and add soy sauce by the spoonful, until reaching the desired taste.

6 Ladle sauce and tteok (if using) over chicken and serve.

Tip During preparation, if the chicken thighs are large, cut into large chunks, keeping some meat on the bones. Cook together for a richer sauce. For an alternative option, use boneless chicken thighs.

samgyetang 삼계탕

ginseng chicken soup

Serves 3 to 4

When I was a kid, I wondered why we ate hot soup, like samgyetang, during the summer. My mom said it helps boost energy and the immune system to help beat the heat. I like eating this dish during the other seasons too, especially the winter months. She pokes fun at me for craving it on cold days, but it has never stopped me. - *Nancy*

Prep Time / 20 min, plus 1 hr to soak

Pressure Cook Time / 20 min

Release / Natural and Quick

1 cup glutinous sweet rice, rinsed and drained until water runs clear

1 (3 to 4 lbs) whole chicken

10 garlic cloves

5 dried jujubes

2 large ginseng roots, fresh or dried

3 scallions, cut in half, plus thin slices for garnish

SESAME OIL DIPPING SAUCE

2 tbsp kosher salt

2 tbsp sesame oil

¼ tsp ground black pepper

VINEGAR DIPPING SAUCE (Optional)

2 tbsp kosher salt

¼ tsp ground black pepper

2 tbsp brown rice vinegar

1 tbsp sesame oil

1 small red or green jalapeño, deseeded and minced

1 In a large bowl, soak the sweet rice in water for 30 minutes, and up to 1 hour.

2 Discard the chicken giblets. Rinse the inside and outside of the chicken and pat dry. Remove the tail and any fatty parts. Fill the cavity with 5 garlic cloves and 2 jujubes. Using skewers or toothpicks, stitch the cavity closed. Tie the legs together with kitchen twine.

3 Drain the sweet rice and place in the inner pot. Place the chicken on top and add the remaining garlic cloves, jujubes, ginseng, and scallion halves into the pot. Add water until it reaches the maximum PC fill line.

4 Turn and lock the lid and move the steam release valve to the sealed position. Select Pressure Cook on High and program for 20 minutes. When the cooking is complete, release pressure naturally for 15 minutes, then quick-release any remaining pressure. Unlock and carefully remove the lid.

5 Discard scallions and carefully transfer the chicken to a large shallow bowl. Using a spoon and skimmer, skim the fat and solids from the broth.

6 In a small bowl, combine the sesame oil dipping sauce ingredients together. In another small bowl, combine the vinegar dipping sauce ingredients together (if using).

7 To serve, remove the twine and skewers from the chicken. Divide the chicken and rice into individual serving bowls and ladle broth on top. Garnish with sliced scallions (if using) and serve with kosher salt and pepper on the side. Use one or both dipping sauces for the chicken.

dak kalguksu 닭칼국수

chicken soup with noodles

Serves 4 to 5

In my childhood home, making kalguksu was a family affair. My mother appointed my dad to dough duty. He would knead the dough, let it rest, knead again, rest, roll out, cut, and place small smooth bundles of noodles on trays. The trays were spread throughout the family room. From time to time, I make handmade noodles and the slightly bouncy texture is addictive. I don't make them often because they are so time-intensive. These days it's easier to purchase pre-made noodles at local Korean grocery stores. - *Nancy*

Prep Time / 20 min
Pressure Cook Time / 17 min
Release / Natural and Quick

1 zucchini, julienned

¼ tsp kosher salt

1 tsp vegetable oil

1 small carrot, peeled and julienned (optional)

1 (3 lb) whole chicken, fat trimmed

½ medium onion, halved

10 garlic cloves

2 scallions, white stems (save green parts for sauce)

3 tsp kosher salt, divided

½ tsp ground black pepper

1 tsp minced garlic

1 ½ tsp sesame oil

1 tbsp guk gan jang (soup soy sauce)

4 servings of fresh kalguksu noodles

SAUCE (Optional)

¼ cup soy sauce

1 scallion, thinly sliced (plus leftover green parts)

1 tsp gochugaru

1 tsp roasted sesame seeds

1 tsp minced garlic

1 tsp sesame oil

1 Place the zucchini in a small bowl and sprinkle kosher salt. Gently mix together. Set aside for 10 minutes.

2 Heat the Instant Pot by selecting the Sauté function on High. Add vegetable oil to the inner pot. When the oil shimmers, add carrots (if using), and sauté until softened. When the carrots have softened, press Cancel and remove from the Instant Pot. Set aside.

3 Squeeze out excess water from the zucchini by hand. Add the zucchini to the inner pot. Select the Sauté function on Low and sauté briefly, about 1 to 2 minutes, then press Cancel. Transfer the zucchini to a dish and set aside.

4 Place the chicken inside the inner pot. Add onion, garlic, and scallion stems. Fill the inner pot with water to the maximum PC fill line.

5 Turn and lock the lid and move the steam release valve to the sealed position. Select Pressure Cook on High and program for 17 minutes. When the cooking is complete, release pressure naturally for 15 minutes. Quick-release any remaining pressure. Unlock and carefully remove the lid.

6 Carefully transfer the chicken to a bowl and let cool. Using a spoon and a skimmer, skim the fat and solids from the broth. (Optional: Strain the broth using cheesecloth and strainer for a clearer broth.) Discard onion and garlic cloves.

7 Once the chicken is cool enough to touch, shred it into bite-sized pieces and place into a bowl. Add 1 teaspoon kosher salt, ground black pepper, and minced garlic to the shredded chicken. Mix together until evenly combined. Set aside.

8 In a small bowl, whisk all the sauce ingredients until well-combined. Set aside for serving.

9 Add guk ganjang and 2 teaspoons of kosher salt (or more to taste) to the broth, then stir. Press Sauté function on High.

10 Place the uncooked noodles into a large bowl and fill with cold water. Loosen the noodles in the water to remove excess starch and drain. Repeat 3 more times and drain well. When the broth is boiling, add the noodles. Boil the noodles until they float to the top and are cooked through, about 3 to 5 minutes. Press Cancel.

11 Divide the noodles into serving bowls. Add zucchini, carrots (if using), and shredded chicken on top. Ladle broth into soup bowls.

12 Serve immediately with sauce on the side.

Tips

- Use chopped scallion greens as a garnish if opting out of the sauce.

- For extra broth, add 1 to 2 teaspoons of guk ganjang for every 1 to 2 cups of water to the broth. Avoid adding too much, guk ganjang will turn the broth dark. As an alternative option, add kosher salt to taste.

- Find fresh kalguksu noodles at Korean and Asian markets or dried versions online. If using dried noodles, cook the noodles in a separate pot for best results.

dak gaejang 닭개장

spicy chicken soup

Serves 4 to 6

July is the hottest month in Korea with temperatures at over 100°F. Sometimes it can rain and stay humid for days on end. Koreans have traditionally consumed chicken soup to regain energy and stimulate appetites during this season. Samgyetang (page 111) is a more commonly known dish but I like making this spicy version. When guk over rice gets boring, I always use spaghetti noodles. The spaghetti and dak gaejang pair well together—call it a modern twist! - *Selina*

Prep Time / 15 min

Pressure Cook Time / 5 min
  plus 10 min to boil

Release / Natural and Quick

½ lb chicken breast

½ lb chicken thigh

1 large onion, halved (½ for stock, ½ sliced)

1 extra-large dae pa (Korean green onion), cut into 2-inch matchsticks (roots saved for stock)

1 tbsp whole black peppercorn, in a strainer bag

2 tbsp cooking oil

¼ small mu (Korean radish), peeled and cut into 2-inch matchsticks

3 tbsp gochugaru

1 cup cooked gosari (fernbrake), rinsed and trimmed into 2-inch pieces

1 cup mung bean sprouts, rinsed

2 tsp fine sea salt

½ tsp ground black pepper

2 tsp minced garlic

2 tbsp guk ganjang (soup soy sauce)

1 tbsp fish sauce

1 In the inner pot, add chicken, onion half, dae pa root, peppercorn strainer bag with 8 cups of water.

2 Turn and lock the lid and move the steam release valve to the sealed position. Select Pressure Cook on High and program for 5 minutes. When the cooking is complete, release pressure naturally for about 5 minutes then quick-release any remaining pressure. Unlock and carefully remove the lid.

3 Remove the strainer bag and discard dae pa root and onion. Transfer the chicken to a dish. Using two forks, shred the chicken into bite-sized strips. Transfer the broth to a large bowl, then rinse the inner pot with warm water.

4 Select Sauté on Low and add cooking oil. Sauté sliced onion and mu until it starts to become translucent, about 4 minutes. Add gochugaru and sauté for another 2 minutes. Select Cancel.

5 Select Sauté on High and add shredded chicken, gosari, mung bean sprouts, and the chicken broth. Add 1 cup of water then bring to a boil for about 10 minutes. When it comes to a high boil, stir in sea salt, black pepper, garlic, guk ganjang, and fish sauce. Boil for another 10 minutes. Add more guk ganjang or sea salt to taste.

6 Serve as is or with cooked spaghetti noodles.

Tip Using a glass lid at Step 4 will speed up the pre-heating and boiling process.

dak hanmari 닭한마리

chicken hot pot with noodles

Serves 3 to 4

If you're wondering how this dish is different from Samgyetang (page 111) or Dak Kalguksu (page 112), I'd say this is a modern family-style version. I'm not as familiar with it since it was popularized by the street corners of Dongdaemoon (East Gate) in Seoul after I moved to the States. I have yet to try the original version but I love that a whole meal can be in a single pot, served for a shared meal. - *Selina*

Prep Time / 20 min
Pressure Cook Time / 10 min
Release / Natural

8 tteokbokki tteok (rice cakes), 2-inch cylinder pieces

8 garlic cloves

1 (2-inch) piece ginger, peeled and thinly sliced

2 tsp whole black peppercorns

1 (2 to 3 lb) whole chicken, excess fat and skin trimmed

1 small yellow onion, halved

2 yellow potatoes, sliced into ¼-inch discs

2 scallions, cut into 2-inch pieces

2 servings fresh kalguksu noodles

DIPPING SAUCE

4 tbsp gochugaru

4 tbsp soy sauce

1 tbsp brown rice vinegar

½ cup grated or puréed yellow onion

1 tsp yellow mustard powder

Special equipment: tabletop burner

1 In a medium bowl, soak tteok in cold water, about 15 minutes, especially if they are frozen and stuck together.

2 Place garlic, ginger, and black peppercorns in a small strainer bag. Add the strainer bag, chicken, onion, and 14 cups of water into the inner pot.

3 Turn and lock the lid and move the steam release valve to the sealed position. Select Pressure Cook on High and program for 10 minutes. When the cooking is complete, release pressure naturally for 10 minutes, then quick-release any remaining pressure. Unlock and carefully remove the lid.

4 In a small bowl, whisk together the dipping sauce ingredients until combined. Set aside.

5 Transfer the chicken to a large shallow pot. Add potatoes, scallions, tteok, and enough broth to cover the contents. Bring to a boil on high heat, until the potatoes are cooked through and tteok are soft, about 10 minutes.

6 Move the pot to a tabletop burner to keep it warm during the meal. Serve family-style, with individual serving bowls and dipping sauce. Add sea salt and pepper to taste.

7 Finish the meal by adding kalguksu noodles to the remaining broth. Cook for about 3 to 5 minutes. Add more broth as needed and serve. The kalguksu noodles will quickly absorb the broth, so eat them as soon as they have cooked to avoid bloated noodles.

Tip Removing excess chicken fat and skin will produce a more clear broth. Purchasing a spatchcocked chicken (backbone removed) can help speed up the cooking process.

chogae guksu 초계국수

cold chicken noodles

Serves 4

Let's Eat is a light-hearted Korean TV series about singlehood and the solo life experience, seen through food. The main character, Gu Dae Hyung, has a deep appreciation for food and shares his food philosophy, often unsolicited. Since watching the show, this simple yet incredibly satisfying noodle dish has become a personal summertime favorite. This dish has a refreshing, familiar, and tangy cold broth like naengmyeon, but the tender chicken, fresh veggies, and egg makes it a completely balanced meal. - *Selina*

Prep Time / 10 min
Pressure Cook Time / 20 min
Release / Natural and Quick

1 cornish hen, skin removed and wing tips trimmed

1 scallion stem

2 tsp whole black peppercorns

4 garlic cloves

4 servings somyeon (wheat flour noodles)

½ Persian cucumber, julienned

4 cherry tomatoes, halved

Egg Jidan (optional, page 74)

CHICKEN SEASONING

1 tbsp minced garlic

1 tbsp minced scallion

½ tsp fine sea salt

½ tsp ground black pepper

BROTH SEASONING
   (per 4 servings)

1 tbsp brown rice vinegar

½ tsp fine sea salt

½ tsp white granulated sugar

½ tsp yeon gyeoja (hot mustard paste)

1 Add cornish hen, scallion stem, peppercorn, garlic, and 12 cups of water to the inner pot.

2 Turn and lock the lid and move the steam release valve to the sealed position. Select Pressure Cook on High setting and program for 20 minutes. When the cooking is complete, release pressure naturally for 10 minutes, then quick-release any remaining pressure. Unlock and carefully remove the lid. Transfer the cornish hen to a dish to cool.

3 Using a spoon and a skimmer, discard the aromatics and skim the fat and solids from the broth. Once the cornish hen is cool enough to touch, shred into bite-sized pieces. Add the chicken seasoning to the shredded cornish hen. Combine well and set aside. Once the broth has cooled to room temperature, store in a freezer-safe container. Freeze about 1 to 2 hours until cold and starts to turn into slush.

4 When ready to serve, remove the broth from the freezer and add the broth seasonings, stirring to combine.

5 In a medium pot, bring 4 cups of water to a boil. Cook somyeon, about 2 to 3 minutes, or according to package's instructions. Use a strainer to rinse the noodles in cold water and drain.

6 Place somyeon in individual bowls and add the broth. Adjust the broth seasoning according to taste (as needed). Garnish with cucumber, tomato, and Egg Jidan (if using) and serve.

dak galbi 닭갈비

spicy chicken stir-fry

Serves 4

Dak Galbi is a chicken stir-fry typically cooked in a large pan with cabbage and goguma. This dish is eaten with lettuce wraps and usually without rice. But when this dish is served at restaurants and as the meal nears its end, the server will add rice to the pan and make fried rice with the leftover sauce and chicken bits. I highly recommend doing this as well, so leave room in your belly! - *Nancy*

Prep Time / 20 min, plus marinating time

Pressure Cook Time / 5 min

Release / Quick

25 tteokguk tteok (coin-shaped sliced rice cakes)

2 tbsp gochugaru

1 tbsp white granulated sugar

2 tbsp soy sauce

3 tbsp rice wine, or sake

2 tbsp minced garlic

1 tbsp oligodang (sweet syrup)

2 tbsp gochujang

2 tsp mild Ottogi curry powder (optional)

1 tsp grated ginger

¼ tsp ground black pepper

1½ lb boneless and skinless chicken thighs, cut into 1½-inch pieces

½ lb green cabbage, cut into bite-sized pieces

1 small goguma (Korean sweet potato), peeled and cut into ¼-inch thick half moons

2 bundles kkaennip (perilla) leaves, stems removed

1 head red leaf lettuce, leaves separated

1 In a strainer, rinse tteokguk tteok and soak them in cold water. Set aside for 10 minutes.

2 In a medium bowl, mix gochugaru, sugar, soy sauce, rice wine, garlic, oligodang, gochujang, curry powder (if using), ginger, and black pepper. Add the chicken to the marinade and combine well. Cover and refrigerate for at least 15 to 20 minutes.

3 Add ¼ cup of water, chicken, cabbage, and goguma to the inner pot and mix together.

4 Turn and lock the lid and move the steam release valve to the sealed position. Select Pressure Cook on High and program for 5 minutes.

5 Cut about 8 to 10 kkaennip leaves into ¼-inch slices. Keep the remaining leaves with the lettuce leaves for the wraps.

6 When the cooking is complete, quick-release pressure manually. Unlock and carefully remove the lid. Press Cancel and select Sauté on High. Drain tteok and add to the inner pot. Add sliced kkaennip leaves. With a large spoon, carefully stir to continue cooking. Avoid breaking the goguma. Cook until tteok are soft, about 2 minutes. If the heat seems too high, set Sauté on Low. Press Cancel when finished.

7 Transfer dak galbi to a large serving dish. Serve with red leaf lettuce and whole kkaennip leaves on the side.

Tip Make a lettuce wrap by layering one lettuce leaf, one kkaennip leaf, and dak galbi.

dak jook 닭죽

chicken porridge

Serves 4 to 6

Jook is a favorite Korean breakfast meal. There are many varieties of jook and some of our personal favorites are featured in this book. I often make dak jook for my kids when they are feeling under the weather. Chicken soup has a universal message of healing and comfort and the creamy smooth texture of jook makes it easier to digest. - *Selina*

Prep Time / 5 min
Pressure Cook Time / 25 min
Release / Natural

1 (1 ½-inch) piece ginger, peeled

4 garlic cloves

2 tsp whole black peppercorns

1 bay leaf

½ lb chicken breast

½ lb skinless, boneless chicken thigh

2 cups short-grain rice, rinsed and drained

Chicken broth, as needed (optional)

White pepper, to taste

1 Add ginger, garlic, black peppercorns, and bay leaf to a strainer bag. Add the strainer bag, chicken, and 12 cups of water to the inner pot.

2 Turn and lock the lid and move the steam release valve to the sealed position. Select Pressure Cook on High and program for 10 minutes. When the cooking is complete, release pressure naturally for 10 minutes, then quick-release any remaining pressure. Unlock and carefully remove the lid.

3 Using a spoon and a skimmer, remove the strainer bag and skim the fat and solids from the broth.

4 Transfer the chicken to a dish. Once the chicken is cool enough to touch, shred the chicken into bite-sized pieces by hand.

5 Return the shredded chicken into the inner pot and add rice. Add more water or chicken broth so that the liquid level is at the 3-quart half-fill line..

6 Turn and lock the lid and move the steam release valve to the sealed position. Select Rice, then Porridge on High and program for 15 minutes. When the cooking is complete, release pressure naturally. Unlock and carefully remove the lid.

7 Season with sea salt and white pepper. Stir until thick and creamy, then serve.

Tip Drizzle Jook Sauce (page 156) on top for extra flavor. Get creative with fixings like sliced scallions and garlic chips.

chicken curry 치킨카레

Serves 4

If you grew up in a Korean immigrant home, you're likely familiar with Ottogi or S&B Golden curry; it's nearly ubiquitous as instant ramen in many households. It was a very common dish in our home because it was a quick and easy dish that the whole family could enjoy. This curry is commonly prepared with the same ingredients, but my mom's unique touch made it special. I loved my mom's soupy curry. It has the perfect runniness to mix with rice. Make sure to serve with chong gak (young radish) kimchi, a bowl of rice, and Miyeok Guk (page 75) for the best combination. It's a classic party of flavors! - *Selina*

Prep Time / 15 min
Pressure Cook Time / 5 min
Release / Quick

1 tbsp unsalted butter

½ medium yellow onion, coarsely chopped

½ lb chicken thigh, rinsed, cut into 1½-inch pieces

½ lb chicken breast, rinsed, cut into 1½-inch pieces

Pinch of fine sea salt

Pinch of ground black pepper

4 Yukon Gold potatoes, cut into ¾-inch pieces

1 medium carrot, peeled and cut into ½-inch pieces

2 tbsp Ottogi curry powder (medium hot)

4 cubes S&B curry roux brick (medium hot)

¼ cup frozen green peas

1 Select the Sauté function on Low and add the butter and onion. Sauté the onion for about 2 minutes and add the chicken. Season with a pinch of sea salt and pepper. Cook the chicken until it's browned lightly on the outside, about 5 minutes.

2 Add the potatoes, carrot, and curry powder. Sauté for another 2 to 3 minutes. Add 2 cups of water.

3 Turn and lock the lid and move the steam release valve to the sealed position. Select Pressure Cook on Low and program for 5 minutes. When the cooking is complete, quick-release pressure manually. Unlock and carefully remove the lid.

4 Select Sauté on Low and add curry cubes and green peas. Slowly stir until the cubes dissolve and the curry thickens, about 3 minutes.

5 Serve with rice and chong gak kimchi, if desired.

Tip For a thicker curry consistency, add more curry roux blocks. For a saltier flavor, add more curry powder or salt to taste.

6

seafood

Hae Mul Jjim, page 124

hae mul jjim
해물찜

seafood stir-fry

124

maeun tang
매운탕

spicy fish stew

125

eundaegu jorim
은대구조림

poached black cod with radish

127

jogae sungaeal miyeok guk
조개 성게알 미역국

seaweed soup with clams & uni

128

jogaetang
조개탕

clams and broth

130

hong hap tang
홍합탕

mussels soup

131

jjamppong
짬뽕

seafood soup

132

mineo jjim
민어찜

steamed sea bass

134

bugeoguk
북어국

dried pollack soup

135

godeungeo jorim
고등어조림

braised mackerel

137

eomuk tang
어묵탕

fish cake stew

138

man neung myelochi yooksu
만능 멸치 육수

multipurpose anchovy stock

139

hae mul jjim 해물찜

seafood stir-fry

Serves 5

This impressive dish takes care of any and all seafood cravings. The Instant Pot gently steams the seafood, which creates a base for the broth. Adding the sauce binds the elements together and makes it simply heavenly. The spicy sauce may look like it could overpower the seafood's delicate tenderness, but it actually enhances it. The listed seafood is a suggestion, use any preferred mix of seafood.

- Nancy

Prep Time / 20 min
Steam Cook Time / 10 min
Release / None

½ **lb cuttlefish or baby octopus**

1 **small crab, cleaned, and cut in half**

⅔ **lb large shrimp (about 12), peeled and deveined**

½ **lb large scallops (10 to 12)**

1 **lb clams, scrubbed**

½ **lb mussels, cleaned and debearded**

½ **lb soybean sprouts**

3 **tbsp gochugaru**

1 **tbsp gochujang**

2 **tbsp rice wine, or sake**

1 **tbsp soy sauce**

1 **tbsp minced garlic**

2 **tsp white granulated sugar**

½ **tbsp cornstarch**

few sprigs of minari (Korean water dropwort) or watercress (optional)

1 Add cuttlefish, crab, shrimp, scallops, clams, mussels, and ½ cup water into the inner pot. Layer the soybean sprouts on top.

2 Turn and lock the lid and move the steam release valve to the sealed position. Select Steam and program for 10 minutes.

3 In a medium bowl, combine gochugaru, gochujang, rice wine, soy sauce, garlic, and sugar. Mix well and set aside.

4 In a small bowl, mix 1 tablespoon of water and cornstarch together and set aside.

5 When the cooking is complete, unlock and carefully remove the lid. The seafood may not be fully cooked through. Press Cancel and select Sauté on High. Push aside the seafood in the center to create a well and pour the gochugaru sauce mixture into the well. Dissolve the sauce concentrate into the broth. Gently mix the seafood and sauce together until evenly coated.

6 Add the cornstarch slurry to the sauce and mix until the liquid has slightly thickened and the seafood is cooked through.

7 Transfer to a serving plate and garnish with minari (if using). Serve immediately.

Tip For an alternative soybean sprouts option, use mung bean sprouts.

maeun tang 매운탕

spicy fish stew

Serves 4 to 5

When my husband, son, and I visited a fish market in Seoul, we picked our fish and went to the restaurant above to have it cooked into maeun tang. The server asked me about the spice level, and I told her in Korean that spicy would be fine. (Maeun translates to spicy.) She hollered to the cook, "One maeun tang, foreigner spicy!" When the stew came out, it was incredibly delicious and insanely spicy—like, burn-my-throat spicy. We laughed and said, "Thank goodness she said "foreigner spicy!" In this recipe, you will have enough sauce to adjust the spice level to your liking. - *Nancy*

Prep Time / 15 min

Pressure Cook Time / 3 min, plus 2 min

Release / Quick

½ lb mu (Korean radish) or daikon, peeled, quartered, and cut into ½-inch thick slices

7 large myeolchi (dried anchovies), heads and guts removed

2 tbsp minced garlic

1 tsp minced ginger

¼ cup guk ganjang (soup soy sauce)

3 tbsp gochugaru

1 tbsp gochujang

1 tbsp doenjang

1 tbsp fish sauce

2 lbs cod or snapper fillets, (or sea bass, pollock, flounder)

½ (12 oz) block firm tofu, cut in ½-inch slices

1 Korean green chili pepper, thinly sliced

1 red jalapeño, thinly sliced

1 small bunch enoki mushrooms, (optional)

2 scallions, sliced diagonally

1 small bunch ssukgat (Chrysanthemum greens), or watercress

1 Place mu pieces in the inner pot.

2 Add myeolchi into a strainer bag and add to the inner pot with mu and 5 cups of water.

3 Turn and lock the lid and move the steam release valve to the sealed position. Select Pressure Cook on High and program for 3 minutes. When the cooking is complete, quick-release pressure manually. Unlock and carefully remove the lid. Discard the strainer bag.

4 In a small bowl, mix the garlic, ginger, guk ganjang, gochugaru, gochujang, doenjang, and fish sauce together until well-combined. Mix in a few spoonfuls of sauce into the broth at a time. Taste and add more, if preferred.

5 Add fish fillets to the pot. Turn and lock the lid and move the steam release valve to the sealed position. Select Pressure Cook on Low and program for 3 minutes. For thin fish fillets, cook for 2 minutes. When the cooking is complete, quick-release pressure manually. Unlock and carefully remove the lid.

(recipe continues)

maeun tang

매운탕

spicy fish stew
(continued)

6 Using a slotted spoon, transfer the fish to a serving bowl. If the fish is not cooked through (depending on the fillet size and thickness), leave the fish fillets in the pot as they will continue cooking in the next step.

7 Select Sauté on High. Sample the broth and add salt and pepper to taste. Adjust the spiciness by adding more sauce or gochugaru. Add tofu, green and red chili peppers, mushrooms (if using), and scallions to the pot and cook for about 3 minutes.

8 When the tofu is heated through, transfer the stew into a serving bowl. Add ssukgat on top and pour the remaining broth on top of the greens. Serve immediately with rice.

Tip To use a whole fish (scales, guts, and fins removed), cut into 2-inch slices. Select Pressure Cook on High and program for 4 minutes. Quick-release pressure when complete.

eundaegu jorim 은대구조림

poached black cod with radish

Serves 4 to 6

I feel incredibly lucky to have a fantastic fish market in my area. When it's stocked with black cod, I purchase it in a heartbeat, without any hesitation. It's also commonly known as butterfish—aptly named—because of its buttery and soft texture...drool. - *Nancy*

Prep Time / 20 min
Pressure Cook Time / 5 min
Release / Quick

¾ lb mu (Korean radish), or daikon, peeled, quartered, and cut into ½-inch thick slices

4 garlic cloves, crushed

1 (2-inch) piece of ginger, peeled and julienned

1 small onion, sliced ¼-inch thick

1 Korean green chili pepper, thinly sliced

1 red jalapeño, thinly sliced

1 cup rice water (see Glossary, page 165), or plain water

¼ cup soy sauce

1 tbsp fish sauce

1 tbsp mirin

2 tbsp gochujang

2 to 4 tbsp gochugaru, adjust to desired spice level

2 tbsp brown sugar

2 tsp sesame oil

2 lbs black cod fillets, cut into 3- to 4-inch wide pieces

2 scallions, sliced diagonally into ½-inch slices

1 Add mu, garlic, ginger, onion, chili pepper, jalapeño, and rice water to the inner pot.

2 In a medium bowl, combine soy sauce, fish sauce, mirin, gochujang, gochugaru, brown sugar, and sesame oil together. Add black cod fillets to the sauce and coat evenly. Place the fillets and remaining sauce mixture in the inner pot.

3 Turn and lock the lid and move the steam release valve to the sealed position. Select Pressure Cook on High and program for 5 minutes. When the cooking is complete, quick-release pressure manually. Unlock and carefully remove the lid.

4 Gently stir in the scallions. Sample the sauce and add salt or gochugaru to taste.

5 Transfer to a serving bowl and serve immediately with a side of rice.

Tips

- For thinner fish fillets, program the cook time to 2 minutes. For fish steaks, cook for 5 minutes.

- For smaller portions, use less fish. All other ingredients and cook time remain the same.

jogae sungaeal miyeok guk

조개 성게알 미역국

seaweed soup with clams & uni

Serves 4

This is a fancy take on good ol' traditional birthday soup (Miyeok Guk, page 75). One of the things that I envy most about living in Korea is the availability of abundant seafood. I love making this version on birthdays since fresh uni and clams are a rare treat. It makes birthdays that much more special. This is also the reason why I need to befriend fishmongers in my area! - *Selina*

Prep Time / 5 min
Pressure Cook Time / 10 min
Release / Quick

1 cup dried miyeok (seaweed), preferably small and precut

2 tsp sesame oil

18 frozen clams, thawed and shucked

1 tbsp guk ganjang (soup soy sauce)

Pinch of fine sea salt

8 lobes fresh uni (sea urchin)

1 In a medium bowl, soak miyeok in room temperature water until it becomes soft, about 5 minutes. Rinse and wash in cold running water. Drain out excess liquid.

2 Select Sauté on High and when warm, add miyeok, sesame oil, and clams to cook for 2 to 3 minutes. Add guk ganjang and cook for 2 to 3 minutes. Add 5 cups of water.

3 Turn and lock the lid and move the steam release valve to the sealed position. Select Pressure Cook on High and program for 10 minutes. When the cooking is complete, quick-release pressure manually.

4 Add salt and adjust the seasoning to taste. Top with fresh uni and serve.

Tip Fresh uni can be found at local fish markets or through local fishmongers.

jogaetang 조개탕

clams and broth

Serves 4

Growing up, I thought spicy foods were always either orange or red. Do not be fooled by the light colored broth in this stew: The chili peppers pack a punch. The first time I tried this dish, I was pleasantly surprised as the broth went down my throat with a zing. It was spicy for me as a kid, but I loved (and still love) the taste of the slightly briny, slightly spicy, light broth. - *Nancy*

Prep Time / 5 min, plus soaking time
Pressure Cook Time / 1 min
Release / Quick

2 lbs littleneck clams, scrubbed

¼ cup kosher salt

1 (4-inch) piece dashima (dried kelp)

2 garlic cloves, minced

1 red jalapeño pepper, thinly sliced

1 Korean green chili pepper, thinly sliced

1 scallion, thinly sliced

Special equipment: kitchen brush

1 In a large bowl, dissolve ¼ cup of kosher salt in 4 cups of cold water. Add the clams and cover in the salt bath. Discard any floating clams. Soak for 30 minutes, up to 2 hours in a cool place.

2 Transfer one clam at a time to a strainer, leaving behind the sand that collects at the bottom of the bowl. Rinse the clams under running cold water and drain.

3 Add dashima and 3 cups of water to the inner pot. Press Sauté on High. Simmer the broth to a boil, about 3 minutes. Using tongs, remove dashima.

4 Add the clams, garlic, jalapeño, and chili pepper to the inner pot.

5 Turn and lock the lid and move the steam release valve to the sealed position. Select Pressure Cook on High and program for 1 minute. When the cooking is complete, quick-release manually. Unlock and carefully remove the lid. The clams should be cooked and shells open.

6 Add salt and black pepper to taste. Transfer to a bowl and top with scallion slices. Serve immediately with rice and banchan.

Tip If some clams have not opened during cooking, transfer open ones to a dish and leave the closed clams in the pot. Let the lid rest on top without turning and locking. Press the Sauté on High and boil for another minute. Discard any clams that do not open.

hong hap tang 홍합탕

mussels soup

Serves 4

I like to make this mussel soup for occasions when I drink soju. I love all types of anju (drinking snacks): from soups to noodles to dried seafood...all delicious. If I get another chance to visit Korea, I'm definitely hitting up pojangmacha (outdoor night pub). - *Selina*

Prep Time / 5 min
Pressure Cook Time / 5 min
Release / Quick

1 ½ lbs fresh mussels

1 Korean red chili pepper, thinly sliced

1 serrano green chili pepper, thinly sliced

4 to 6 garlic cloves, halved lengthwise

2 tbsp soju, or cooking wine

2 scallions, stems cut into 3-inch pieces, plus thin slices for garnish

1 tsp lemon juice

2 tsp fine salt

1 Wash the mussels in cold running water and agitate them against each other to remove any dirt or sand. By hand, debeard mussel hairs attached to the shells.

2 Add 5 cups of water, mussels, chili peppers, garlic, soju, and scallion stems to the inner pot.

3 Turn and lock the lid and move the steam release valve to the sealed position. Select Pressure Cook on High and program for 5 minutes. When the cooking is complete, quick-release pressure manually. Unlock and carefully remove the lid.

4 With a slotted spoon, remove the scallions and transfer the mussels to a serving platter. Season the broth with lemon juice and sea salt. Stir and ladle the broth over the mussels.

5 Garnish with sliced scallion greens (if using) and serve.

Tip During rinsing, if the mussels release excess sand, cover with sea salt water and soak for about 1 hour.

jjamppong 짬뽕

seafood noodle soup
Serves 4

As a kid, whenever our family went to a Chinese-Korean restaurant, I always ordered the rich jjajangmyeon and never the spicy jjamppong. I would peer at my dad's jjamppong and think: some day, I'll advance to jjamppong and slurp the tender noodles from that fiery seafood broth. I graduated, of course, and this is one of my favorite dishes. - *Nancy*

Prep Time / 30 min
Pressure Cook Time / 2 min
Release / Natural and Quick

½ lb mussels, cleaned and debearded

1 lb littleneck clams, scrubbed

½ lb large shrimp (about 10), shelled and deveined

½ lb squid, cleaned and cut into bite-sized pieces

4 servings of jjajangmyeon noodles (Chinese-style wheat noodles)

⅓ cup vegetable oil

¼ cup gochugaru

2 tbsp minced garlic

2 tsp minced ginger

4 scallions, cut into 2-inch pieces

2 tbsp soy sauce

1 tbsp gochujang

½ lb pork tenderloin, cut into bite-sized pieces

½ yellow onion, thinly sliced

1 carrot, thinly sliced

1 zucchini, halved lengthwise and thinly sliced

6 medium Napa cabbage leaves, cut into 2-inch pieces

6 medium shiitake mushrooms, stems removed and sliced

8 cups Man Neung Myeolchi Yooksu (page 139), or kelp or chicken stock

1 Measure and prepare all ingredients before cooking. The stir-frying portion moves quickly, so make sure to have ingredients ready and nearby. Prepare the seafood and refrigerate until ready to use.

2 Bring a large pot of water to boil and cook the noodles according to the package. Rinse the noodles in cold water and drain well. Divide the noodles into serving bowls.

3 Select the Sauté function on Low and add vegetable oil. When the oil is shimmering, add gochugaru, garlic, and ginger. Sauté for about 20 seconds, until the garlic and ginger are golden in color and gochugaru is a shade darker. Quickly add scallions, soy sauce, gochujang, and the pork. Stir-fry until the pork is nearly cooked through and slightly pink, about 1 to 2 minutes. Add the onion, carrot, zucchini, cabbage, and the mushrooms. Stir everything together until well-combined. Press Cancel and add man neung myeolchi yooksu.

4 Turn and lock the lid and move the steam release valve to the sealed position. Select Pressure Cook on High and program for 2 minutes. When the cooking is complete, release pressure naturally for 5 minutes, then quick-release any remaining pressure. Unlock and carefully remove the lid. Taste the broth and add salt to taste.

5 Select the Sauté function on High. Add mussels, clams, shrimp, and squid. Simmer until the seafood is cooked and the mussels and clam shells have opened. Discard any shells that have not opened. Press Cancel to avoid overcooking.

6 Ladle the soup over the noodles in serving bowls and serve immediately.

mineo jjim 민어찜

steamed sea bass

Serves 4

While my husband and I were dating, we once walked into a hole-in-the-wall Korean restaurant in downtown San Francisco. We were both excited to recognize mineo jjim on the menu, a dish that is not commonly found in restaurants outside of Korea. It was the best fish dish we'd ever had. The fresh sea bass was seasoned, jam-packed with flavors and spices, it made a lasting impression. I don't recall the restaurant's name or if it even still exists today but this is my attempt to recreate the magical dish, purely from memory! - *Selina*

Prep Time / 10 min
Pressure Cook Time / 10 min
Release / Quick

1 ½ lb sea bass, or croaker, cleaned, head and gut removed

½ cup soy sauce

½ tbsp doenjang

3 tbsp gochugaru

2 tbsp white granulated sugar

1 tbsp minced garlic

2 tsp ginger juice

½ small mu (Korean radish), peeled and cut into ½-inch thick slices

1 scallion, chopped

¾ lb ssukgat (Chrysanthemum greens), stems removed

1 Cut the fish into 3 evenly sized chunks. Using kitchen tweezers, remove visible fish bones. Lightly season with salt.

2 In a medium bowl, whisk soy sauce, doenjang, gochugaru, sugar, garlic, and ginger juice until well-combined. Set seasoning sauce aside.

3 With a vegetable peeler, shave off any hard edges from mu chunks. Lay mu to cover the bottom of the inner pot. Place the fish on top and add the seasoning sauce with ½ cup of water.

4 Turn and lock the lid and move the steam release valve to the sealed position. Select Pressure Cook on High, program for 10 minutes. When the cooking is complete, quick-release pressure manually. Unlock and carefully remove the lid.

5 Garnish with scallions and ssukgat, and serve.

Tip For ssukgat substitute, use parsley or cilantro.

bugeoguk 북어국

dried pollack soup

Serves 4

Bugeoguk is known as a hangover cure, or a sobering soup. And since there are no distinctions between Korean meals, this dish can be eaten for breakfast, lunch, or dinner. A typical Korean breakfast includes a bowl of hot, clear soup, a bowl of rice, and a few banchan. I love making this soup the night before and eating it the next morning. Had a rough night of too many drinks? Trust me, you will love this soup in the morning. If you know, you know. - *Selina*

Prep Time / 10 min
Pressure Cook Time / 7 min
Release / Natural and Quick

2 tsp perilla oil

2 cups bugeo (dried pollock), 2-inch long pieces

⅓ small mu (Korean radish), or daikon, peeled and sliced into bite-sized pieces

½ (12 oz) block firm tofu, cut into small cubes

1 scallion, chopped

1 egg, whisked

2 tsp fine sea salt

½ tsp white pepper

1 Korean red chili pepper, thinly sliced (optional)

1 Select Sauté on Low, add perilla oil, bugeo, and mu to cook, about 2 to 3 minutes. Press Cancel and add 5 cups of water.

2 Turn and lock the lid and move the steam release valve to the sealed position. Select Pressure Cook on Low and program for 7 minutes. When the cooking is complete, release pressure naturally for about 5 minutes, then quick-release any remaining pressure.

3 Select Sauté on Low. Add tofu and scallion. When the broth comes to a boil, add the egg mixture. Gently stir to cook the eggs, about 2 minutes. Add fine sea salt and white pepper, then stir.

4 Garnish with red chili peppers (if using) and serve.

Tip Bugeo is also known as hwangtae. Golden yellow in color, bugeo is sold in pouches and labeled as hwangtae bugeo.

godeungeo jorim 고등어조림

braised mackerel

Serves 4

Growing up, grilled fish made a regular appearance at the dinner table. Mackerel was our choice—or rather, I'd say, my mom's choice. The smell of fried mackerel was irresistible. I remember fish bones getting caught in my throat and eating spoonfuls of rice or gulping water to push them down. So parents: prior to cooking, try to remove visible bones. The tail parts have less bones and better for serving to young children. Godeungeo jorim is super savory and the chunky radish soaks up all the flavors from the braised spicy sauce. Some might even say the radish is the scene-stealer of the dish.

- Selina

Prep Time / 10 min, plus 30 min to soak

Pressure Cook Time / 10 min

Release / Natural

2 mackerel, heads, tail, and guts removed

½ cup soy sauce

½ tbsp doenjang

2 tsp gochugaru

1 tbsp white granulated sugar

2 tbsp minced garlic

2 tsp ginger juice

½ small mu (Korean radish), peeled and cut into big chunks

1 scallion, chopped

1 red chili pepper (optional)

1 Using kitchen tweezers, remove any large fish bones. Soak the mackerel in rice water (see Glossary, page 165), about 30 minutes.

2 In a small bowl, whisk soy sauce, doenjang, gochugaru, sugar, garlic, and ginger juice until well-combined. Set seasoning sauce aside.

3 With a vegetable peeler, shave off any hard edges from the mu chunks. Layer the mu chunks across the bottom of the inner pot. Lay the fish on top, then add the seasoning sauce and 1 cup of water.

4 Turn and lock the lid and move the steam release valve to the sealed position. Select Pressure Cook on High and program for 10 minutes. When the cooking is complete, quick-release pressure manually. Unlock and carefully remove the lid.

5 Select Sauté on Low, spoon the remaining sauce from the pot onto the fish, and let it boil, 2 to 3 minutes.

6 Garnish with scallions and red chili pepper (if using) and serve.

Tip If the fish is on the meatier side, score the flesh with a knife to help absorb more sauce during cooking.

eomuk tang 어묵탕

fish cake stew

Serves 4 to 6

I like buying the assorted package of fish cakes because everyone has their favorites, so having variety is good. Making the broth in the Instant Pot can save time, which leaves more time to accessorize the dish! I typically have a pack of fish cakes in my freezer, so to be perfectly honest, I like to toss fish cakes into this easy broth for a fast weeknight meal. - *Nancy*

Prep Time / 10 min
Pressure Cook Time / 5 min
Release / Natural and Quick

15 large myeolchi (dried anchovies), heads and guts removed

1 large dashima (dried kelp), about 3x6-inch piece

½ small mu (Korean radish), peeled, quartered, and cut into ½-inch slices

1 lb eomuk (fish cakes)

1 tsp minced garlic

1 tbsp guk ganjang (soup soy sauce)

2 scallions, thinly sliced

DIPPING SAUCE (Optional)

¼ cup soy sauce

½ tsp white granulated sugar

½ tsp gochugaru

1 tsp roasted sesame seeds

1 tsp sesame oil

½ tsp minced garlic

1 green chili pepper, diced

1 scallion, thinly sliced

1 Place myeolchi in a strainer bag. Add the strainer bag, dashima, mu, and 8 cups of water to the inner pot.

2 Turn and lock the lid and move the steam release valve to the sealed position. Select Pressure Cook on High and program for 5 minutes.

3 Rinse eomuk in water to remove excess oil and drain well. Cut eomuk into bite-sized pieces.

4 When the cooking is complete, quick-release pressure manually. Unlock and carefully remove the lid. Discard the anchovy stock bag.

5 Select Sauté on High. Add the garlic, guk ganjang, and eomuk to the broth and cook until heated through, 2 to 3 minutes.

6 Season with salt and pepper to taste and add scallions.

7 In a small bowl, mix the sauce ingredients together for dipping (if using).

8 Serve eomuk tang with rice, banchan, and dipping sauce.

Tip For a simpler dipping sauce, use Yangnyeom Ganjang (page 154).

man neung myeolchi yooksu

만능 멸치 육수

multipurpose anchovy stock

Makes 8 cups

Man neung myeolchi yooksu is to Korean cuisine as chicken stock is to the western world. It's a base used in many Korean dishes, versatile and easy to make. Don't skip toasting myeolchi for extra depth of flavors and clean tasting results. No fishy stock, please. - *Selina*

Prep Time / 5 min
Pressure Cook Time / 30 min
Release / Quick

20 large dried myeolchi (dried anchovies), heads and guts removed

½ small mu (Korean radish), cut into large chunks (leave skin and roots)

1 medium onion, cut in half (leave skin and roots)

10 precut dashima squares (dried kelp)

1 Select Sauté on Low and add myeolchi to the inner pot. Toast myeolchi until the edges are light brown, about 3 minutes. Add mu, onion, dashima, and 8 cups of water to the pot.

2 Turn and lock the lid and move the steam release valve to the sealed position. Select Pressure Cook on High and program for 30 minutes. When the cooking is complete, quick-release pressure manually. Unlock and carefully remove the lid.

3 Pour the liquid through a strainer into another large vessel to remove any remains or debris for a clear broth.

4 Cool to room temperature before refrigerating or storing in the freezer. Freeze the stock for up to one month.

Tips

- To make a vegetarian or vegan stock, substitute myeolchi for dried shiitake mushrooms.

- Dashi pouches are also available to purchase in Korean groceries. Use 2 to 3 packs for the same results. Some contain dried fish, make sure to check the ingredient contents on the packaging.

7
snacks & sweets

Jjimjilbang Eggs, page 142

jjimjilbang eggs
찜질방 구운계란
korean sauna baked eggs
142

yakbap
약밥
sweet rice cake
143

gukmul tteokbokki
국물 떡볶이
soupy spicy rice cakes
145

pat icebar
팥 아이스바
red bean popsicles
146

danpatjuk
단팥죽
sweet red bean porridge
148

shikhye
식혜
sweet rice punch
149

sujunggwa
수정과
cinnamon ginger punch
150

jjimjilbang eggs 찜질방 구운계란

korean sauna baked eggs

Serves 3 to 4

Jjimjilbang is a public bathhouse, or spa. You can enjoy different types of saunas and spa treatments: kiln saunas, steam rooms, massages, hot and cold bathtubs. But the best thing that comes to mind when I think of jjimjilbang is the variety of food and snacks available. If you are a fan of Korean dramas, eating baked eggs, sipping on sweet slushy Shikhye (page 149), and wearing sheep's ear-shaped towel hats may be a familiar scene. My mom and I recently visited a Korean spa in Los Angeles and we spent hours and hours chatting and eating snacks as we warmed our bodies on the ondol (heated stone) floors. Now I can recreate the experience at home using the Instant Pot! - *Selina*

Prep Time / 2 min
Pressure Cook Time / 1 ½ hr
Release / Natural

1 tbsp fine sea salt

1 tbsp vinegar

6 large eggs, at room temperature, rinsed

1 In the inner pot, mix 1 ½ cups water with sea salt and vinegar. Insert the steamer rack.

2 Place the eggs on the steamer rack. Cook 6 to 8 eggs at a time to avoid stacking eggs.

3 Select Pressure Cook on High and program for 1 hour and 30 minutes. When the cooking is complete, quick-release pressure manually. Unlock and carefully remove the lid.

4 Cool for about 1 to 2 minutes before peeling. The eggs are best served hot.

Tip Baked eggs do not need to be soaked in cold water and will peel easily.

yakbap 약밥

sweet rice cake

Serves 6 to 8

Yakbap, or also known as yaksik, is often spotted on the dessert table at Seollal (New Year's Day) or Chuseok (Thanksgiving Day). Traditional Korean fare doesn't have a distinct category for baking or dessert but making sweet rice cakes plays a big role in the cuisine. As a Korean cook, I hope to someday take a deep dive into this area of Korean culture. Yakbap is also an easy snack to transport around and especially good for long hikes. It's easy to digest and is a good energy-boosting source. Individually wrapping Yakbap in bite-sized serving sizes is convenient for travel. - *Selina*

Prep Time / 5 min plus 1 to
    4 hrs to soak
Pressure Cook Time / 8 min
Release / Natural and Quick

2 cups sweet rice, rinsed and drained

2 tbsp sesame oil, divided

2 tbsp dark soy sauce

⅓ cup brown sugar

1 tbsp ground cinnamon

4 dried jujubes, pitted and cut in thin slices

6 roasted chestnuts, cut in quarter chunks

1 tbsp pine nuts

Special equipment: 8x4-inch loaf pan

1 Rinse and soak the rice in a large bowl of cold water for 1 hour and up to 4 hours (the longer the better). Drain well.

2 Coat the inner pot with about 1 tablespoon of sesame oil. Add soaked sweet rice, dark soy sauce, brown sugar, cinnnamon, sesame oil, and 1¼ cups water. Stir until well-combined. Lay the dried jujubes, chestnuts, and pine nuts on top.

3 Turn and lock the lid and move the steam release valve to the sealed position. Select Pressure Cook on Low and program for 8 minutes. When the cooking is complete, release pressure naturally for 15 minutes, then quick-release any remaining pressure.. Unlock and carefully remove the lid. Stir the rice mixture.

4 Line the loaf pan with parchment paper. Transfer the rice into the loaf pan and keep tightly packed. Once cooled, cut Yakbap into approximately 3x2-inch squares and serve. To store, individually wrap with plastic cling wrap and freeze immediately to preserve freshness (up to 4 weeks).

5 Serve with hot tea or pack for traveling.

Tips

- Add 1 tablespoon of raisins and/or pumpkin seeds at Step 1 for extra texture and flavors.

- Allow frozen yakbap to thaw naturally to room temperature before eating. Avoid reheating in the microwave.

gukmul tteokbokki 국물 떡볶이

soupy spicy rice cakes

Serves 2 to 3

In my faint memory, tteokbokki was the very first dish I purchased on my own. It was at a small neighborhood hole-in-the-wall eatery on my way home from school while growing up in Seoul. I still remember the place: O-Shi-O Tteokbokki. It means Please Come, Tteokbokki. I would spend all my allowance there to eat tteokbokki. The owner was super kind to students and always gave us extra rice cakes. I recently learned it still exists and I would love to go back to visit someday. It would be like traveling back to my childhood.
- *Selina*

Prep Time / 5 min plus 10 min cooking (not including boiling eggs)

Pressure Cook Time / None

Release / None

1 lb tteokbokki tteok (rice cakes), 2-inch cylinder pieces, fresh or packaged

2 tbsp gochujang

1 tbsp fine gochugaru

1 tbsp soy sauce

1 tbsp white granulated sugar

4 to 5 precut dashima (dried kelp) pieces

3 dried shiitake mushrooms

2 sheets eomuk (fish cake), cut into triangles

2 scallions, cut into 2-inch matchsticks

2 tbsp oligodang (sweet syrup)

1 tsp dashida (beef bouillon powder)

6 hard-boiled quail eggs, peeled

4 fried mandu (dumplings) (optional)

4 gim mari (fried glass noodle seaweed rolls) (optional)

1 Using a colander, rinse and separate tteok in cold running water, then drain.

2 In a small bowl, whisk gochujang, gochugaru, soy sauce, and sugar until well-combined. Set sauce mixture aside.

3 Select Sauté on Low and add dashima squares, mushrooms, and 3 cups of water. Bring to a boil, about 5 minutes. Using a skimmer or spoon, remove dashima and mushrooms. Add the sauce mixture and stir until dissolved into the stock.

4 When the sauce comes to a boil, add eomuk and scallions to cook, about 2 to 3 minutes. Add tteok and keep stirring until tteok are soft, about 2 minutes. Add oligodang and dashida to finish cooking.

5 Transfer tteokbboki to a serving platter or a dish. Add eggs, and with a ladle, generously top with sauce. Serve with fried dumplings or gim mari (if using) for dipping into the sauce.

Tips

- Adjust spice levels by using a milder type of gochugaru and gochujang.

- Substitute tteok with mil tteok (wheat flour rice cakes).

- If using frozen tteok, soak in a bowl of cold water, about 15 minutes before separating.

pat icebar 팥 아이스바

red bean popsicles

Makes 6

I love red bean desserts. I am addicted to eating tteok filled with pat anggeum (red bean paste), I devour pat bbang (red bean filled pastry), and during the summers, pat ice bars are next level obsession. Most red bean popsicles at the market are filled with sugar, corn syrup, sweetened cream (yes, more sugar!), and flavor enhancers for the beans. I'm not really trying to skimp on the sweetness factor here, but I've removed the corn syrup and simplified with easy ingredients. Once frozen, the popsicles will taste less sweet, so don't freak out if the liquid mixture tastes very sweet before freezing. I mean, you can add a little more condensed milk if you think you need to up the sweetness. I promise I won't look. - *Nancy*

Prep Time / 5 min
Pressure Cook Time / 17 min
Release / Natural and Quick

½ cup dried adzuki beans, or red beans, rinsed and drained

1 ⅓ cup whole milk

½ cup condensed milk

Pinch of kosher salt

Special equipment: Blender, popsicle mold, popsicle sticks

1 Place the rinsed adzuki beans into the inner pot and add 2 cups of water.

2 Turn and lock the lid and move the steam release valve to the sealed position. Select Pressure Cook on High, and program for 17 minutes. Turn off the Keep Warm function. When the cooking is complete, release pressure naturally for 5 minutes, then quick-release any remaining pressure. Unlock and carefully remove the lid.

3 Drain the cooked adzuki beans and place the beans in a blender. Add whole milk and blend together until smooth.

4 Add the condensed milk, kosher salt, and blend until well-combined. Pour the mixture into popsicle molds. Insert popsicle sticks and place in the freezer until frozen (about 4 to 8 hours) before serving.

danpatjuk 단팥죽

sweet red bean porridge

Serves 4 (appetizer or dessert servings)

This is a simplified version of the red bean porridge typically eaten during Dongji (winter solstice). Add Saealsim (page 56) and season with sea salt to serve as a meal. This dish can also be turned into a porridge by adding rice. Patjuk can be made savory or sweet, depending on preference. This recipe is written to be served as an appetizer or dessert. - *Selina*

Prep Time / 30 min
Pressure Cook Time / 12 min
Release / Natural

1 cup red adzuki beans, rinsed and drained

1 tbsp sweet rice flour (Mochiko brand)

2 tbsp white granulated sugar

Special equipment: Blender

1 In a bowl of water, cover and soak the beans for about 30 minutes and drain. Pick out any broken beans.

2 Place the beans in the inner pot with 3 cups of water.

3 Turn and lock the lid and move the steam release valve to the sealed position. Select Pressure Cook on High and program for 12 minutes. When the cooking is complete, release pressure naturally. Unlock and carefully remove the lid. Let the steam out and let cool.

4 The beans should be soft and tender enough to mash. Using a slotted spoon, add the beans to a blender and add about ½ cup of bean water. Blend until smooth.

5 Select Sauté on Low. Pour the blended bean mixture and 1 cup of water to cook for about 3 to 5 minutes. Add sweet rice flour to thicken and keep stirring until it is smooth and silky.

6 Add sugar and stir for another 3 minutes. Serve immediately.

shikhye 식혜

sweet rice punch

Serves 4 to 6

Shikhye is one of two very traditional drinks, alongside Sujunggwa (page 150). Shikhye is a sweet rice drink typically served at the end of a meal. I don't have much of a sweet tooth but after a hot and spicy meal, sipping on shikhye has a cooling effect and is very enjoyable. Make it at home and let the Instant Pot do the work overnight while you are getting your night's rest. It will be ready to drink the next day.
- *Selina*

Prep Time / 15 min
Pressure Cook Time / 8 hrs
  (fermentation)
Release / None

1 cup fine malt powder
½ cup cooked white rice
2 tbsp white granulated sugar
1 tsp ginger juice

Special equipment: fine mesh
  strainer bag

1 In a fine mesh strainer bag, add fine malt powder. Let the powder dissolve with 4 cups of room-temperature water in a large bowl, until the water turns cloudy and malt sediments sink to the bottom, about 10 to 15 minutes. Squeeze the bag occasionally to help the malt powder dissolve.

2 Pour the sweet malt liquid through a strainer into the inner pot and discard the remains. Add rice and 6 cups of water, and stir to mix.

3 Select Keep Warm on High for 8 hours overnight. Select Sauté on Low and add sugar and ginger juice. Bring to boil for about 5 minutes and press Cancel. Let the liquid cool to room temperature.

4 Chill in the fridge for 2 or more hours and serve cold. Store in a pitcher with lid.

Tip Use strainer bags with drawstrings to securely close the top. At Step 1, hold the strainer bag with one hand and grab the bottom with the other to squeeze out excess liquid.

sujunggwa 수정과

cinnamon ginger punch

Serves 6

Sujunggwa always gives me warm holiday feelings. The cinnamon and ginger pairing reminds me of using red wine and citrus for mulled wine. This drink is served on Seollal (New Year's Day) with Korean holiday snacks like rice cakes, dried persimmons, yakgwa (sugar cookies), and shared blessings. I also love to make this drink during winters as a cold and flu remedy. When your throat feels a little scratchy, you know it's time to make this. - *Selina*

Prep Time / 3 min
Pressure Cook Time / 1 hr
Release / Natural

8 cinnamon sticks

½ medium ginger root, peeled and sliced

8 dried jujubes

⅓ cup brown sugar

Pine nuts (optional)

2 dried jujubes, thinly sliced (optional)

1 Add 6 cups of water with cinnamon sticks, ginger, and jujubes to the inner pot.

2 Turn and lock the lid and move the steam release valve to the sealed position. Select Pressure Cook on Low and program for 60 minutes. When the cooking is complete, release pressure naturally. Unlock and carefully remove the lid.

3 Using a strainer, remove cinnamon sticks, ginger, and jujubes. Select Keep Warm and add brown sugar. Stir to melt, about 1 to 2 minutes.

4 Serve hot, topped with pine nuts and dried jujube slices (if using) or serve cold after chilling in the fridge.

Tip Adjust sugar amounts according to preference.

8

sauces

Yangnyeom Ganjang, page 154, Bibimjang, page 154,
and Ssamjang, page 155

yangnyeom ganjang

양념간장

dipping soy sauce

154

bibimjang

비빔장

bibimbap sauce

154

ssamjang

쌈장

*sauce for korean bbq &
lettuce wraps*

155

kongnamul bap
yangnyeom jang

콩나물밥 양념장

kongnamul bap sauce

155

saeujeot jang

새우젓장

salted shrimp sauce

156

jook sauce

죽 양념장

porridge sauce

156

samgyetang sauces

삼계탕소스

157

man neung ganjang

만능간장

multipurpose soy sauce

158

man neung
yangnyeom jang

만능양념장

multipurpose red chili sauce

159

gang doenjang

강된장

thick soybean paste for rice

160

yangnyeom ganjang 양념간장

dipping soy sauce

Makes about ½ cup

This is a simple, soy sauce based dipping sauce. For a spicy version, add gochugaru for some extra heat. Use yangnyeom ganjang as a dipping sauce for dumplings, Korean savory pancakes, or Eomuk Tang (page 138). - *Nancy*

¼ cup soy sauce

2 tbsp brown rice vinegar, or rice vinegar

1 ½ tsp white granulated sugar

1 ½ tsp roasted sesame seeds

1 tsp sesame oil

Pinch of ground black pepper

1 scallion, thinly sliced

½ to 1 tsp gochugaru (optional)

In a small bowl, whisk all ingredients together until well-combined.

bibimjang 비빔장

bibimbap sauce

Makes 1 cup

The ultimate bibimbap sauce. Make and drizzle generously over a large bowl of Samsaek Namul (page 23), rice, and a preferred protein for a healthy and delicious bowl of bibimbap (page 24). - *Selina*

½ cup gochujang

1 tsp minced garlic

1 tsp white granulated sugar

1 tbsp sesame oil

1 In a small bowl, combine gochujang and 1 ½ cups of water. Mix to create a thin consistency.

2 In the following order, add: garlic, sugar, and sesame oil.

3 Whisk ingredients together until well-combined.

ssamjang 쌈장
sauce for korean bbq & lettuce wraps
Makes about 1 cup

This sauce is best known for accompanying lettuce wraps at Korean BBQ. It's also great for dipping crudités, like cucumber slices and peppers! - *Nancy*

½ cup doenjang
⅓ cup gochujang
2 tbsp sesame oil
¼ cup minced onion
2 tsp minced garlic
1 scallion, thinly sliced
2 tbsp roasted sesame seeds
1 tbsp white granulated sugar

In a medium bowl, mix all ingredients together until well-combined.

kongnamul bap yangnyeom jang 콩나물밥 양념장
kongnamul bap sauce
Makes about ½ cup

This soy sauce based sauce used for Kongnamul Bap (page 42) can be used for any dish that gets tossed together. I'll often add this sauce to a simple bowl of rice and fried egg, and mix them together for a meal. - *Nancy*

¼ cup soy sauce
1 tsp gochugaru
1 tsp white granulated sugar
1 tsp roasted sesame seeds
2 tsp minced garlic
2 tsp sesame oil
2 scallions, thinly sliced

In a small bowl, add all ingredients and mix together until well-combined.

saeujeot jang 새우젓장

salted shrimp sauce

Makes about ¼ cup

Salty and briny, this sauce is known for accompanying Bossam (page 89). Saeujeot pairs well with pork, so use saeujeout jang to supplement any simple grilled pork dish. I often put tiny amounts of saeujeot on spoonfuls of jook to complement the porridge's plain savory flavors. - *Nancy*

3 tbsp saeujeot (salted shrimp)

1 tsp gochugaru

1 tsp roasted sesame seeds

In a small bowl, add all ingredients and mix together until well-combined.

jook sauce 죽 양념장

Makes about ½ cup

This is a light and thin soy sauce based sauce that can top any savory jook. Use this sauce as a salt substitute. - *Selina*

¼ cup soy sauce

1 tbsp brown rice vinegar

2 tsp white granulated sugar

In a small bowl, add all ingredients with 2 tablespoons of water and whisk together until the sugar has dissolved.

Tip Top jook with sauce and drizzle sesame or perilla oil for added nuttiness.

samgyetang sauces 삼계탕 소스

Makes 2 servings

Use one or both sauces to dip the stewed chicken from Samgyetang (page 111). The sauces can also be used for Korean-style cooked meats that are prepared without any seasoning, like roast gui (grilled beef slices) and grilled samgyeopsal. - *Nancy*

SAMGYETANG DIPPING SAUCE

2 tbsp kosher salt

2 tbsp sesame oil

¼ tsp ground black pepper

SAMGYETANG VINEGAR DIPPING SAUCE

2 tbsp kosher salt

¼ tsp ground black pepper

2 tbsp brown rice vinegar

1 tbsp sesame oil

1 Korean green chili pepper or jalapeño, deseeded and finely chopped

1 In a small bowl, whisk all the samgyetang dipping sauce ingredients together until well-combined.

2 In another small bowl, whisk all the samgyetang vinegar dipping sauce ingredients together until well-combined.

man neung ganjang 만능간장

multipurpose soy sauce

Makes 4 cups

This man neung, or mat ganjang, is a soy sauce simmered with aromatics, spices, and sweet flavors. It's dense and strong and should only be used for cooking, like banchan or braising meats. I have a small batch of this brew in my fridge at all times. I love that man neung ganjang is jam-packed with flavors, so additional flavor boosters aren't necessary when cooking with this soy sauce. - *Selina*

Prep Time / 5 min
Pressure Cook Time / 15 min
Release / Natural

3 cups soy sauce

½ yellow onion, (roots and skin intact)

½ cup precut dried shiitake mushrooms

4 precut dashima (dried kelp) pieces

4 garlic cloves

2 tbsp ginger juice

¼ cup honey

1 Add ingredients and 1 cup of water to the inner pot, stir to mix well.

2 Turn and lock the lid and move the steam release valve to the sealed position. Select Pressure Cook on Low and program for 15 minutes. When the cooking is complete, release pressure naturally. Unlock and carefully remove the lid.

3 Using a strainer, remove the aromatics and let the sauce cool to room temperature. Store in a glass jar and refrigerate for up to 6 weeks.

Tips

- Man neung ganjang can be used in many banchan like Myeolchi Bokkeum (page 27) and Gaji Namul (page 34).

- For extra flavor boosts, add other Korean aromatics like 1 dae pa (Korean green onion), ¼ cup chung ju (cooking sake), 1 tablespoon yuja chong (yuzu syrup), or 1 cup gadalangeo po (bonito flakes).

man neung yangnyeom jang

만능양념장

multipurpose red chili sauce

Makes ¼ cup to start

Start by adding ingredients with equal parts, and adjust to taste before scaling portions. For 2 to 4 servings, start with 2 tablespoons of each ingredient. This chili sauce is used as a marinade for meats like Dak Galbi (page 118) or as a seasoning sauce for stir-fried banchan like Maneul Jjong (page 39). - *Selina*

Soy sauce

Gochugaru

Gochujang

Mirin

White granulated sugar

Minced garlic

In a small bowl, whisk all sauce ingredients together until well-combined.

gang doenjang 강된장

dense soybean paste (for over rice)

Serves 4

Is it true that your taste buds start to dull as you age? My palate now gravitates towards dishes that I didn't particularly like growing up. I find them increasingly comforting and satisfying in both flavor and affection, and gang doenjang is one of those dishes. This dense version of soybean stew (see Doenjang Jjigae, page 78), packed with flavor, depth, and textures, can be eaten topped over rice. The word 'gang' means strong. Yes, quite strong in flavor but you come back for it again and again. This sauce goes well with mixed barley rice and chive kimchi. It's super gang delicious! - *Selina*

Prep Time / 10 min
Pressure Cook Time / 5 min
Release / Natural and Quick

½ lb pork (belly, shoulder or ground), chopped into small cubes

Pinch of fine sea salt

Pinch of ground black pepper

1 tsp ginger juice

1 tbsp mirin

2 tsp cooking oil

4 tbsp doenjang

2 yellow potatoes

¼ onion, chopped

1 tbsp minced garlic

½ (12 oz) block firm tofu, cut into ¼-inch cubes

2 scallions, thinly sliced

1 serrano pepper, chopped

1 Korean red chili pepper, chopped

1 Combine pork with salt, pepper, ginger juice, and mirin in a medium bowl. Set aside.

2 Select Sauté on Medium, drizzle cooking oil, and cook the marinated pork until browned. Add doenjang and ¾ cup of water to the inner pot and stir until it dissolves into the water, about 5 minutes.

3 Add potatoes, onion, garlic, and tofu to the inner pot.

4 Turn and lock the lid and move the steam release valve to the sealed position. Select Pressure Cook on High and program for 5 minutes. When the cooking is complete, release pressure naturally for 5 minutes, then quick-release any remaining pressure. Unlock and carefully remove the lid.

5 Add scallions, serrano, and red chili peppers for garnish and stir. Best served with barley rice and chive kimchi.

Tip For a quick chive kimchi, cut 2 (¼ lb) chive bunches into 2-inch long pieces. Season with 2 teaspoons each of gochugaru, fish sauce, white granulated sugar, and sesame oil. Add more gochugaru for spice.

glossary

Anchovies/Kelp dry stock bags, or dashi pack 멸치다시팩**.** A stock bag filled with prepped myeolchi and precut dashima. Sometimes they contain small dried shrimp. Sold in Korean markets and online. You can make your own bags by putting myeolchi and dashima in a large tea bag or tied up in a cheesecloth.

Brown rice vinegar 현미식초**.** Made from fermented brown rice and is light to dark brown in color. More nutrients than regular rice vinegar. Can be substituted with white rice vinegar.

Caramel syrup 카라멜 시럽**.** Made with part molasses and water and can be found in Asian markets. For an alternative option, use a combination of dark soy sauce and brown sugar.

Ssukgat 쑥갓 **(chrysanthemum greens).** Also known as crown daisy, ssukgat leaves are flat and leafy. Used in soups, stews, and side dishes. Substitute with flat leaf parsley in a pinch.

Chunjang 춘장 **(black bean paste).** Korean-style fermented black bean paste made of soybeans, wheat flour and caramel. It is salty, earthy, and slightly bitter. Cook to remove some of the bitterness before eating. Some chunjang comes precooked to save time. It is not the same as Chinese black bean paste, so make sure to find chunjang.

Chwinamul 취나물 **(dried aster scaber).** Fragrant leafy vegetable found growing wildly in many mountain regions in East Asia. Usually found dried in Korean markets.

Dae pa 대파 **(bunching onion).** Dae pa looks like a very large scallion except sweeter and more fragrant. It is used to flavor soups and stews and different from leeks. Do not substitute dae pa with leeks. If you cannot find dae pa, use scallions.

Daechu 대추 **(jujubes).** Small fruits with pits, eaten fresh or dried. All daechu used in this book are dried and used as a sweetener or garnish.

Dangmyeon 당면 **(sweet potato starch noodles).** Chewy and bouncy noodles made from sweet potato starch. Also called glass noodles or Korean vermicelli.

Dark soy sauce 중식 진간장**.** Thicker and darker soy sauce that is slightly sweet. Aged for longer periods of time with molasses. No real substitution for dark soy sauce, but you can sweeten regular soy sauce with a little bit of molasses and a pinch of sugar.

Dashima 다시마 **(dried kelp).** Thick sheets of dried kelp used for many soup bases. Can be found in long sheets or precut for cooking. Also can be found labeled as Japanese kombu.

Doenjang 된장 **(fermented soybean paste).** A paste made from soybeans and salt that has been fermented for months. Doenjang is thick, salty, nutty, sharp, and a bit funky. This one sauce packs a punch with complex and incredible deep flavors.

Dried red chili peppers 건고추. Dried, whole, Korean red chilis. When deseeded and ground, it makes gochugaru.

Fish sauce 액젓. Light brown sauce made from fermented fish. Complex and deep gamchilmat (umami) flavors used to season many dishes from kimchi, banchan, main entrées, soups and stews.

Ganjang 간장 **(soy sauce).** Soy sauce made from fermented soybeans, a roasted grain, and salt. We like using Sempio brand soy sauces.

Gochugaru 고춧가루 **(red chili pepper flakes).** Fine or coursely ground, deseeded sun-dried Korean red chili peppers. Store gochugaru in an airtight bag or container in the freezer to maintain freshness. When we list gochugaru in the ingredients in this book, we are referring to coarse gochugaru. Fine gochugaru (powder form) will be stated.

Gochujang 고추장 **(red chili pepper paste).** Red chili pepper paste made of Korean chili powder, fermented soybean powder, glutinous sweet rice powder, and salt. Gochujang is spicy, slightly pungent, sweet, and very bold. Comes in different levels of spice ranging from mild to super hot.

Gosari 고사리 **(fernbrake).** Young fernbrake stems. Found presoaked or dried at Korean markets, and used in soups and banchan.

Guk ganjang 국간장 **(soup soy sauce).** A by-product of doenjang, it is lighter in color and saltier than regular soy sauce. It is very strong and bold in flavor; great for seasoning soups and stews. If you do not have guk ganjang, use 1 teaspoon of fish sauce for every tablespoon of guk ganjang.

Jajangmyeon noodles 짜장면 **(wheat flour noodles).** Wheat flour noodles used for jajangmyeon and jjamppong. Sometimes found in Korean markets labeled as "Chinese-Style Noodles." These are thinner than udon, but use udon noodles as a substitute.

Kalguksu 칼국수 **(flour noodles).** Kalguksu means knife cut noodles in Korean. These flour noodles can be found fresh at the Korean markets. Dried versions can be found at the markets or online. If you cannot find kalguksu, use udon noodles as an alternative.

Kkaennip 깻잎 **(perilla leaves).** Perilla leaves are a member of the mint family. They look similar to shiso leaves, but more aromatic and stronger in flavor. Kkaennip is found in Korean markets but difficult to find elsewhere. Shiso leaves can be used as a substitute in soups, stews, and toppings, but not as a standalone banchan dish. If you cannot find kkaennip or shiso for a soup or stew dish, then omit.

Kongnamul 콩나물 **(soybean sprouts).** Soybean sprouts commonly used in Korean cooking. Slightly nutty in flavor with crispy stems, kongnamul is found in Korean and some Asian markets. It is difficult to substitute kongnamul with anything else, so unless stated to use mungbean sprouts, use only kongnamul.

Korean eggplant 가지. Known as gaji, this eggplant is elongated with medium-thick skin and few seeds. Sweeter than common Italian or globe eggplant. Substitute with Chinese or Japanese eggplant.

Korean green or red chilis 청양고추, 홍고추. Known as gochu, Korean chili peppers are green or red and vary in heat level. Usually about 3 to 4 inches long with pointy ends. When the green ones ripen, they turn red on the vine. If you cannot find Korean gochu, substitute with serrano peppers or jalapeños.

Korean pears 배 (**Asian pears**). An apple-shaped pear that is crisp, sweet, juicy, and fragrant. Used as sweeteners and also as a tenderizer in marinades. Also known as Asian pears, if Korean pears are not available, substitute with Bosc pears.

Minari 미나리 (**water dropwort**). Korean water dropwort have crispy stems and leaves that look similar to parsley. It is also known as Korean watercress, so if minari cannot be found, use watercress. Not all water dropworts are edible as some species are toxic, so best to stick with finding this specific varietal at the market!

Mirin 미림 (**Korean cooking wine**). A sweet cooking wine used for marinades, sauces, tenderizing, and removing unpleasant odors from meats and fish. The alcohol in mirin enhances flavors in dishes. You can substitute mirin by combining a 3:1 ratio of sake and sugar. Dry sherry or sweet marsala wine can be used in a pinch.

Miyeok 미역 (**dried seaweed for soups**). Dried sea mustard (seaweed) for soups. Can be found labeled under Japanese wakame.

Mu 무 (**Korean radish**). Korean radishes are firm and pale green at the top and fades to white. Although it is similar to daikon, it is heavier, spicier, and has more water content than daikon. If you cannot find mu, substitute with daikon.

Myeolchi 멸치 (**dried anchovies**). They come in different sizes. Large myeolchi are used for broths and smaller ones are typically used in banchan. Discard heads and black innards from large myeolchi before using, otherwise it can leave a bitter taste. No need to do this to small myeolchi; they will not affect the flavor of the dish.

Napa cabbage 배추. Oblong-shaped cabbage with light green leaves (yellow inside). Also known as Chinese cabbage or celery cabbage. It is used widely in East Asian cuisines.

Oligodang 올리고당 (**sweet syrup**). Also known as oligosaccharide, oligodang is used as a sweetener in sticky glazes. Less sweet than corn syrup or sugar. Can be substituted with rice syrup or honey.

Ottogi curry powder 오뚜기 카레가루. Popular Korean curry powder brand. It is different from curry powder found in the spice aisle. If you cannot find Ottogi curry powder, use S&B curry powder.

Oyster sauce 굴소스. A dark, thick, syrupy, salty, and slightly sweet sauce made with oyster extract, salt, sugar, and a thickener like cornstarch. This flavorful sauce is sweet, savory, loaded with gamchilmat (umami), and not super pungent like fish sauce. Oyster sauce can be found in most stores. There are vegetarian versions of oyster sauce made from mushrooms that can be found in stores or online.

Perilla oil 들기름. Oil made from cold-pressed perilla seeds. This oil is nutty, earthy, and fragrant. It can be used in cooking and marinades, but we also love using it as a finishing oil. It does not have a long shelf life (around six months), so buy small bottles if you know you won't be using much.

Perilla seed powder 들깨가루. Ground roasted perilla seeds used to enhance and add depth of flavor to dishes. For substitution, grind roasted sesame seeds.

Plum extract syrup 매실청. Known as maesil chung, plum extract is syrupy and sweet. Often used as a sweetener, or sugar replacement for its nutritional qualities. Often used in marinades and dipping sauces.

Rice syrup 쌀조청. Sweet syrup made from rice and barley malt powder. It is not as sweet as corn syrup and sugar. Sometimes we like to substitute it with maple syrup, but you can use less sugar if needed.

Rice vinegar 쌀식초. Sweet and delicate, rice vinegar is made from fermented rice. Substitute with apple cider vinegar if needed.

Rice water 쌀뜨물. Rice water is the water saved from rinsing uncooked rice. Do not use the water from the first or second rinsing since they remove most of the dust from the rice. Save the water from the third or fourth rinse for cooking.

Rice wine or cooking sake 청주. Cheongju in Korean, this clear liquor made from rice is used for seasoning, sauces, and marinades. It has some sweetness, but not as sweet as mirin. Use sake if you cannot find cheongju.

S&B curry roux block 카레고형. Commonly found as S&B Golden Curry in stores and comes in three different spice levels: mild, medium, and hot.

Somyeon 소면 (wheat flour noodles). Very thin wheat flour noodles found in the dried noodle section of Asian markets and some mainstream markets. They are also called somen in Japanese, and sumian in Chinese.

Tteok 떡 (rice cakes). Korean rice cakes made from rice flour. There are many different ways to prepare tteok, from savory to sweet. The two main types used in this book are tteokguk tteok (sliced tteok in oval shapes), and tteokbokki tteok (cylindrical shape tteok around 2 inches in length).

Yeon gyeoja 연겨자 (hot mustard paste). Made from finely ground mustard powder, this hot mustard paste packs a punch. Be careful or it can knock you to your knees and clear your sinuses, so use a little bit at a time. This type of heat is not spicy, but closely resembles horseradish and wasabi.

cooking tables

High-Altitude Cooking

When you are at altitudes higher than 2000 feet, adjust your cooking time by using this chart:

At or Above	Increase Cook Time	Or Multiply By
2000 ft	5%	1.05
3000 ft	10%	1.1
4000 ft	15%	1.15
5000 ft	20%	1.2

Sous-Vide Cooking Temperatures and Times
For Ribeye or Strip Steaks

Doneness	Temperature	Cooking Time Range
Rare	120°F–128°F	1 to 2 ½ hours
Medium Rare	129°F–134°F	1 to 2 ½ hours
Medium	135°F–144°F	1 to 4 hours
Medium Well	145°F–155°F	1 to 3 ½ hours
Well Done	156°F and up	1 to 3 hours

It is not recommended to sous vide steaks for more than 2 hours. General rule of thumb: if the steak is 1½-inches thick, cook for 1½ hours. If the steak is 2-inches thick, cook for 2 hours.

recipe index

acknowledgments

Nancy:

My biggest thanks to my husband, Brad. You believe in me more than I do—and although I think you're a little cuckoo for it sometimes, I am incredibly grateful with all my heart that you always have my back. To my 엄마 and 아빠 for dedicating their lives to giving us a better life. My sister, Denise, who I can talk to every day and who will listen to all of my stuff. My son, Ben, whom I hope will learn to make all of these recipes. To Selina, for agreeing to go on this cookbook journey with me. It's been so much fun working together. Thank you to Caroline, Meg, and Jaymar who worked so hard on this book. I feel especially lucky to have this amazing team to work with and for believing in this project. Most of all, I want to thank all the women in my family. Many of my stories and memories start with watching you in the kitchen and tasting your food. All of the recipes, tips, and ingredients began with you, and you've inspired so many of these recipes for me.

Selina:

I would like to thank my boys Raymond, Nathan, and Tyler for supporting me through my difficult career change and long transition into the food industry. Quietly and patiently believing in me that I could do it—and most of all, eating every leftover from countless recipe testings! I want to thank my appah for giving me the legendary Lee family taste buds and my umma for teaching me that family's happiness can start in the kitchen. I also want to thank my late grandmother, halmoni, for showing me that presentation does matter and even home-cooked meals can be served beautifully. Last but not least, huge thanks to Nancy for encouraging me to contribute to this book and to Caroline, Meg, and Jaymar for all your hard work. I am so proud of us all.

about the authors

Beginning her career in piano performance and music composition, **Nancy Cho** followed her passion for art and food as an editor and recipe developer for *Anthology* magazine, where she sought flavors and ingredients inspired by memories of her childhood. She is the author of *The Easy Asian Cookbook for Slow Cookers*, a cookbook featuring recipes of East, Southeast, and South Asian cuisines for slow cookers. Nancy also works as a photographer and stylist and has photographed several books and cookbooks for clients such as Penguin Random House. She lives in the San Francisco Bay Area with her husband, and son.

⌨ nancycho.design
◎ @fmly.style

Selina Lee was born in Seoul, Korea, and moved to U.S. with her family when she was a teenager. Growing up, she had an interest in art and studied graphic design. She worked at *Korea Central Daily* as an advertising designer and worked for Lionbridge Technologies, Inc. as a senior publishing manager. Looking for a way to engage her growing interest in Korean cooking, she launched a series of in-person classes called Banchan Workshop in 2014. That interest developed into a deep passion and she decided to pursue a career in food. Currently, she is working as a menu and recipe developer for local restaurants and food companies. She lives in Oakland, California with her husband and two teenage boys.

⌨ selinaslee.com
◎ @selina.s.lee

Follow our cookbook & recipe adventures: @kipcookbook @KoreanInstantPotCookbook

CPSIA information can be obtained
at www.ICGtesting.com
Printed in the USA
LVHW020310230921
698448LV00006B/95